"The message of this book is age old but most people don't awaken to life until a disaster strikes. Jampolsky's book can make you aware of your options, and when inspiration and information come together transformation occurs."

—Bernie Siegel, M.D., author of
Love, Medicine, and Miracles and *Prescriptions for Living*

"Smile for No Good Reason is hands down the most accessible and practical book ever written on Attitudinal Healing. If you buy it and read it, you will keep it forever."

—Hugh Prather, author of
The Little Book of Letting Go and *Spiritual Notes to Myself*

"This is a delightful book that guides people through the daily stresses of life with hope and optimism."

—Caroline Myss, best-selling author of
Why People Don't Heal and How They Can
and *Anatomy of the Spirit*

Other books by Dr. Lee Jampolsky

*Healing the Addictive Mind: Freeing Yourself
from Addictive Patterns and Relationships*

The Art of Trust: Healing Your Heart and Opening Your Mind
with Gerald G. Jampolsky, M.D.:

*Listen to Me: A Book for Men and Women
About Father-Son Relationships*

SMILE

For No Good Reason

Simple Things
You Can Do
to Get Happy
NOW

DR. LEE JAMPOLSKY

HAMPTON ROADS
PUBLISHING COMPANY, INC.

Cover design by Frame25 Productions
Cover art © Images.com/Corbis

Hampton Roads Publishing Company, Inc.
1125 Stoney Ridge Road
Charlottesville, VA 22902
434-296-2772
fax: 434-296-5096
e-mail: hrpc@hrpub.com
www.hrpub.com

If you are unable to order this book from your local
bookseller, you may order directly from the publisher.
Call 1-800-766-8009, toll-free.

Library of Congress Catalog Card Number: 00-105255

ISBN 978-1-57174-574-3

First Hardcover Edition: October 2000

10 9 8 7 6 5 4 3 2 1

Printed on acid-free paper in the United States

DEDICATION

In honor of my father, Dr. Gerald Jampolsky, who
founded Attitudinal Healing over thirty years ago,
and in 2005 received the Pride in the Profession
Award from the American Medical Association.
Through this book it is my hope, privilege,
and purpose to uniquely contribute to his work,
and the work of countless others from the Centers
for Attitudinal Healing throughout the world.

This book is also in memory of author Richard
Carlson, whose book *Don't Sweat the Small Stuff*
served as the inspiration for this one.

Table of Contents

PRINCIPLE NUMBER SIX:

We can learn to love ourselves and others by forgiving rather than judging.

PRINCIPLE NUMBER SEVEN:

We can become love finders rather than fault finders.

PRINCIPLE NUMBER EIGHT:

We can choose and direct ourselves to be peaceful inside regardless of what is happening outside.

PRINCIPLE NUMBER TWELVE:

We can always perceive ourselves and others as either extending love or giving a call for help.

ACKNOWLEDGMENTS

I am most moved by simple writings from the heart which reach to the depths of the human spirit. It is this that I strive to do. I would like to acknowledge the many authors who have done this so well and have inspired me to write this simple book. Specifically, I wish to acknowledge Neale Donald Walsch, Hugh Prather, Richard Carleson, Richard Bach, the Dalai Lama, Jerry Jampolsky, and Hal Zina Bennett: You have been my teachers in how to communicate truths by touching the heart.

In deep gratitude to my daughters, Jalena and Lexi, who continue to teach me so much about smiling.

I equally acknowledge all those who have brought, and will bring, peace and laughter to a world that could use a few more smiles coming from a loving heart. This includes you.

INTRODUCTION

Attitudinal Healing has touched the hearts of dying children and adults, eased the pain of citizens ravaged by war, redirected Fortune 500 companies, captured the attention of world leaders, assisted medical experts in major universities, been welcomed by Nobel Peace laureates, and yet most people have still not heard of Attitudinal Healing. This, in part, is because there is nothing commercial about it. It is a quiet wisdom for those who want it. In the high-tech information age such basic knowledge can easily go unnoticed.

This book presents clear and concise ways—that you can *begin* right now—to *begin* living a happier and more meaningful life. You will learn to feel more peaceful and be more productive by replacing the automatic ways you react from fear with new perceptions of yourself and the world.

A primary teaching of Attitudinal Healing is: *Nothing needs to change in your life situation or the world in order for you to have peace of mind.* At first, such a notion may seem implausible. This idea is foreign to the typical way of thinking, which states "If you're unhappy, change something in your life. Change jobs, buy something new, find a different relationship."

It is easy to become sidetracked and stressed by a multitude of little tasks and problems, and to lose sight of what really matters. In this increasingly complicated world, what is needed is to remind yourself of what is most precious. This book offers simple and practical ways to be happy by approaching life with a different attitude.

Have you noticed that the changes you make in your life are often only short-term fixes? Regardless of how you modify your life, do stress and conflict soon creep back in? Changing life circumstances without addressing your thinking is like painting over rust: It will look great for a while, but eventually the old rust will slowly break through the new paint. By addressing your attitudes, nothing more and nothing less, whatever changes you make will contribute to your lasting happiness rather than lead to another disappointment or failure.

Attitudinal Healing is a way of having happiness without having to change your social status, religion, spouse, or the amount in your bank account. Attitudinal Healing is a way to go through your day responding to life's challenges with peace of mind rather than with fear, anger, and guilt. It has helped thousands of people and can now help you.

My father, Dr. Gerald Jampolsky, as a means of helping children and their families suffering from catastrophic illness, originally developed Attitudinal Healing in the seventies. The principles of Attitudinal Healing were originally inspired by *A Course In Miracles*, a three-volume set of books published by the Foundation for Inner Peace. I began working with these ideas in 1977 while in graduate school, and they continue to guide and improve my life. I have also seen the principles help transform the lives of people from diverse backgrounds, cultures, and religions.

This book is divided into one section for each of the twelve principles of Attitudinal Healing. Each section contains vignettes to help apply the principles to daily living. It is my hope the short writings will resonate with something deep within you, and that you will find yourself smiling for no good reason.

1

The essence of our being is love.

Love releases us into the realm of divine imagination, where the soul is expanded . . . Love allows a person to see the true angelic nature of another person, the halo, the aureole of divinity.

Thomas Moore, in *Care of the Soul*

WHATEVER THE PROBLEM, LOVE IS IN THE SOLUTION.

Life can appear to be an endless series of problems to be solved—some big, some small, some insurmountable—all calling for a different solution. You may even be facing some right now.

Attitudinal Healing offers another way of looking at problems (and the world) by focusing on the one solution to all your challenges: Your *attitude* in solving any problem is far more important than the particular action you might take. When you approach a perceived problem with a defensive or angry attitude, even if you arrive at the desired solution, you will not have peace of mind. What good does it do you to solve problems if you never find happiness?

If you are compassionate in your approach to all tasks in life, believing that all "problems" contain valuable lessons, you will find peace of mind. Instead of being a constant "problem solver" become a "love giver." This one shift can change your life.

Life is not as complicated as you have made it with your endless list of problems. Attitudinal Healing is based on three simple truths:

1. There are really only two emotions: love and fear.

2. There is really only one problem: the belief that you are separate from God, humanity, and nature.

3. There is really only one solution: discovering that the essence of your being is love.

When your mind is fearful, which it can easily become accustomed to being, you hold on to guilt and resentments from the past, and anticipate problems in the future. This creates a life where, even though you may accomplish a good deal, consistent happiness is impossible. It is important to see that your guilt and resentments are causing you pain and limiting your growth, success, and happiness. Only by seeing the effects of guilt will you be willing to see the alternative.

Whatever the problem, love is the solution. You may be saying, "Well, my problem is that my mortgage is late. How is love going to pay it?" Or, "My problem is that I just got fired from my job. How is love going to be the solution?" Or, "I am alone and want a relationship. Whom do I have to love?"

When these types of situations happen in your life, you can become very narrow in your thinking. All of your energy goes into the crisis at hand, and peace of mind escapes you. In approaching any problem or upset that you have there are two truths that will help you direct your life toward happiness. These may not necessarily put money in the bank, have your boss rehire you, or deliver your soul mate to your door, but they *will* put peace in your mind. Then, regardless of the situation, you will find happiness.

The two truths that will direct your mind toward peace and give you the ability to get the most out of all situations are:

1. I can choose to be peaceful no matter what is happening.

2. Life's problems have nothing to do with my true identity. I am one with God, and my essence is love.

Reminding yourself of these truths on a regular basis throughout the day will be a beginning in taking charge of your thinking, and thus your life. Practicing them when confronting a challenging life situation will make you immune to the ups and downs of the world.

Knowing your peace of mind is up to you, not the world, is the most powerful and secure state of mind you can achieve.

It is hard to look at children and not see innocence. If you allow them to, they will teach you everything about love.

I have a friend named Michael who is four years old. Michael has a rare chromosome disorder and is delayed in some of his cognitive development in areas such as speech. I was speaking with his mother and I asked how his speech was coming. In a loving way she let me know that Michael is doing just fine at *being who Michael is*. I realized that my emphasis on the importance of language, instead of other forms of communication, kept me from seeing and fully appreciating Michael. She went on to tell me that though he doesn't talk much he kisses and hugs quite a bit, and he doesn't discriminate as to who receives his enthusiastic and spontaneous affection. Thus there are some surprised strangers receiving large and loving embraces.

After speaking with Michael's mom, I realized that I would benefit from talking less and indiscriminately loving more. Michael never sees a world full of problems to be solved. He sees a world full of people to be loved.

> *The essence of yourself as a child still lives in you, innocent and full of love. Let a child re-introduce you to yourself.*

DECIDE WHAT YOU
ARE A STUDENT OF.

When people enroll in college or other institutions, they decide what courses they would like to take, assumably because they have interest in the subject. It would not make much sense, or be conducive to learning, to randomly go from class to class each day with no direction or purpose.

Think of your life as a place of education where you have the opportunity to choose what you want to learn. Imagine you can choose between two curriculums: One is taught at Fear State, the other at Love University.

To attend Fear State, the only requirement is for you to believe that you are separate from God and therefore your essence is *not* love.

To attend Love University, your only requirement is for you to believe there just might be another way to go through life. No matter what you may have done in the past you will never be rejected from Love U. Also, Love University allows transfers from Fear State at any time, no questions asked.

The curricula at the two schools are quite different and lead to very different realities and experiences. Fear State is based on the philosophy of the ego, which teaches that you are alone and separate in a cruel and harsh world. Love University is founded on the truth that all beings are created in love, and that this love is within you now.

Take a look at the courses each offers, and decide where you want to spend your time learning. Note that Fear State describes its courses in a way that might initially sound attractive. Like any relentless recruiter, Fear State tries to sell you by saying that following its path will ultimately make you safe, powerful, and secure. When reading its course offerings, ask yourself if the recruiter just might be trying to pull the wool over your eyes.

FEAR STATE COURSE OFFERINGS

Fear 101. The Use of Guilt and Judgment:
This course teaches numerous ways to beat oneself and others up about things the student may have done in the past, and about who one believes one is. The premise is that one does this so as not to make further mistakes.

Fear 102. The Use of Blame:
This unique course offers the student ways to avoid just about anything. It teaches that if one doesn't feel peaceful, all one need do is find what is wrong in the external world and blame it. This course is a prerequisite for Fear 105.

Fear 103. The Use of Time:
Students will learn how to dwell on problems and will learn that trust is a foolish thing. In the second part of the course, the student will learn a variety of ways to worry about the future. None of the material teaches about the present, because, to the fearful mind, it is dangerous and uncontrollable.

Fear 104. Desire and Scarcity, the Greatest Motivators:

The student will be taught that the more one has and accomplishes, the happier one will be. Emphasis is on the belief that as long as the student wants more, the student will be motivated to achieve. Scarcity will be taught by demonstrating if one gives away what is believed to be important, one will have less.

Fear 105. Control All and Be Safe:

The central teaching of this course is that if one can always be right, one can always be happy. The first part of the course teaches that if one can control others one will achieve great success. The second part shows how to use guilt, intimidation, fear, domination, manipulation, conditional love, and criticism to get what it is that one thinks one wants.

LOVE UNIVERSITY COURSE OFFERINGS

Love 101. Acceptance:

This course teaches that the only thing one can really change is one's own mind. The student is taught to accept what cannot be changed, and change what can be, thereby achieving peace of mind.

Love 102. Forgiveness:

Through seeing no value in holding on to guilt the student discovers the essence of all beings is love. This is the foundation of forgiveness.

Love 103. The Use of Time:

Participants will learn how to discover love by letting go of the past and ceasing to worry about the future. Participants remove all limitations from themselves and others by practicing the core teaching: "Now is the only time there is. This instant is for giving and receiving love."

Love 104. Abundance:

Participants learn that giving and receiving are one in truth. Through ongoing demonstrations, everyone joyfully learns the important equation that what is most important, love and compassion, increase as we give them away.

Love 105. Service:

Participants learn that the greatest source of joy comes from sharing Love. Through service, students learn that assisting others in loving ways gives purpose and meaning to their existence.

Each minute of every day you are deciding upon what you want to learn. Both Fear State and Love University are possible choices, but only one is worthy of your investment. The more you can consciously turn your back on the loud recruiter of Fear State and walk toward the gentle guidance of Love University, the more you will discover the dividends of joy, happiness, and self-acceptance.

You choose your own curriculum.
Do you want to be a student
of love or a student of fear?

> # SPEND MORE OF YOUR LIFE TRYING TO UNDERSTAND OTHER PEOPLE'S VIEWS THAN TRYING TO SELL THEM ON YOUR OWN.

What did you want most as a child? To be loved? And what could most effectively communicate that you were loved? Was it not to be listened to with interest and caring? Though the world might seem much more complicated as an adult, nothing has changed in terms of your most basic needs. There is no greater gift you can give a person than listening to them.

Despite popular opinion, the goal of listening is *not* to figure out how the other person is wrong and how you can make them see it your way. Nor is it to figure out what the problem is and fix it. The goal of authentic listening is to love.

People are so busy in our culture that lack of listening is epidemic. One of the most common complaints in couples' therapy is, "I just want to be heard. He/she doesn't understand me." Teenagers often state, "I am tired of only hearing what I do wrong. You have no idea what my life is really like." Younger children act out because they experience their parent's lack of listening. Employees often know their company well and have good ideas, yet rather than being listened to, they are often handed a new policy to follow.

Officials elected to represent the people often forget to listen and instead they promote agendas of their own.

Listening can be mistaken for doing nothing. This is because you can believe that taking some sort of physical action is always necessary. Listening authentically is active, and is one of the most powerful actions you can initiate in your life.

Try a little experiment. Instead of taking some physical action, focus on actively listening more. *Active listening means that you listen to other people with the full intention of understanding them.* For this experiment, let go of any criticism you might have of the other person. Don't try to figure out any solutions to what they are saying. Simply listen. Your eye contact, relaxed body posture, and unhurried mood all communicate, "I want to know your perspective and your experience." If you give verbal responses, let them be centered on trying to understand the other person, as opposed to arguing or offering your opinion or advice.

This experiment can be challenging because really listening requires slowing down and being present. It is worth the effort because there is no greater gift, especially to those people whom you most love.

Practice active listening and other people will feel loved and accepted by you. And, you will feel like you were just given wings.

If you were dining in a restaurant and the waitperson kept putting more food on your plate, you would likely say you were full. Does it not make sense to do the same when your being—your emotions, intellect, and spirit—is on overload? Know when your plate is full and you will be much happier.

In today's fast pace, few encouraging words are given in the workplace for a balanced and thoughtful life, in which one has clear priorities of family, physical, spiritual, and mental health. A common attitude has become "the more stress you can handle the better." Compliments are given to those who look haggard while saying, "Boy, what a rough day! I had twelve hours of nonstop work."

Eight common signs of having too full a plate are:

1. People close to you suggest you slow down.

2. There are no more people close to you.

3. The mere thought of working less brings on anxiety.

4. Rather than relaxing on vacation you bring along "just a little" work or have a long list of things to do or sights to see. Or, you begin to feel anxious on returning from a holiday.

5. You spend less and less time doing activities that are important to you.

6. Little, insignificant things easily annoy you.

7. Your body reacts with frequent illness.

8. You die young.

Some years ago in New York City it was discovered by chance how stress could begin to feel like what is normal. A noisy above-ground portion of an existing subway was re-routed away from the windows of many apartment houses. Surprisingly, rather than all of the tenants being able to sleep better, they were no longer able to sleep well at all. Peace and quiet were keeping them up all night! It turned out that most of them were waking up at the exact times the train *was supposed* to be going by. Over the years, they had become so used to the stress of the noise they now felt out of sorts without it.

It is possible that you live a life so constantly full of stress that you have become acclimated to it. Even when your plate is full you may continue to take on more. In fact, you may be so used to stress that when it is not there it feels like something is wrong.

You may believe that you have no choice other than to live with your current level of stress. Think again. Your stress can be reduced. Begin by:

- Knowing when your plate is full and responding accordingly.

- Seeing that the purpose of all communication is to extend love.

It is remarkable how stress melts away when one sees that the purpose of every interaction is to love. You make room for this to happen in your life by not taking too much on.

You can choose to stop living a life
where you take on more and feel less.
This is one foundation of a spiritual path.

YOU ARE MORE IMPORTANT THAN YOUR "TO DO" LIST.

Chances are excellent that the day you die your "to do" list will not be empty. You could either kill yourself trying to get it all done, or never start living because there is always something else to do first. There is another way.

Not only are *you* more important than your list of things to do, so are other people in your life. It is easy to put off relating to your self, spouse, kids, friends, and animals—decide not to. Decide to relate.

At least three times every day take a moment and ask yourself what is *really* important. Have the wisdom and the courage to build your life around your answer.

I recently came across the following quote that puts priorities in perspective. I don't know where it originated, but its simple wisdom gets my attention.

If you knew today was your last day to live who would you call, and what would you say? What are you waiting for?

Upon contemplating this question, you may begin to realize how much of your life has been spent thinking that things other than love would give you what you want. This is an easy mistake to make. Looking about the world what do you see? A multitude of movies filled with themes of revenge. Endless advertising which not-so-subtly suggests that some new material possession will give you what you want. Relationships devoted to the idea that you should give only if you know what you will get in return. Children experiencing the face of a computer more than the loving face of their parents.

How different your life becomes when you direct it toward God and see nothing as more important than love.

Fear can create "cataracts of the mind," where seeing through the eyes of love becomes difficult. Cataracts of the mind are made of ancient resentments, unreleased guilt, relentless fear, and endless thoughts of scarcity. When you look through this occluded lens, how could you possibly see the love that is really there?

In seeking love you don't seek something elusive. Love is always available. Yet it is easy to close the door to happiness because of the belief that something other than love offers what you want.

Fostering relationships which support your spiritual path is another way of creating a place to receive the gifts of God. There is incredible power when two or more people join together with the sole purpose of support and love. It is the stuff from which miracles are made.

I have a dear friend who is going through tremendous pain and grief right now. Her initial reaction was to close her heart, get busy with work and family responsibilities, and go on. However, she knew from experience, as do you and I, that this does not bring happiness. It is perhaps survival, but who wants survival that ends in continuous loneliness and unhappiness? My friend decided to do something different this time. She is reaching out and finding those who can love and support her. Some of these people she knows well, others she has yet to meet. The important thing is that she is deciding to do something other than isolate and withdraw because of her pain. She is deciding to receive love. For some of us the act of receiving is the largest of our challenges and takes tremendous courage.

To both learn and demonstrate that love offers everything you want, I suggest:

> Spend some time (start with five minutes and work up) every morning and evening reminding yourself that what God wills for you is perfect happiness.
>
> Spend at least one hour a week with an individual or a group whose members are also

reminding themselves that they want what love offers.

Once a year, spend a couple of days with a group or a person who is devoted to learning the lessons love has to offer.

Love offers everything that I want and love is always available to me.

CREATE A PERSONAL
MISSION STATEMENT.

Have you noticed that one day something can set you off and another day you take the same thing in stride? This is because the way you react is completely dependent upon what thoughts you hold in your mind.

A sailboat without a keel and rudder will be blown wherever the winds and tides direct. In the same way, without a stated purpose the winds of life can easily blow you where they will. You may end up feeling that you have few choices, or worse, feeling like a victim.

One of the first things an effective new business will do, or an established one that desires new direction and success, is create a mission statement. An effective mission statement is short and direct. It is the rudder of the vessel, keeping it on track in both challenging and successful times.

Similarly, creating a personal mission statement can give your life new meaning and keep you from falling into familiar patterns or habits. To begin, set aside some time and write down whatever comes to your mind when you ask yourself, "What is important to me? How do I want to live my life?" Next, write a few summary sentences that embody all you have said on your list. Sharpen it up and you have a mission statement.

About five years ago, by asking myself the above questions, I developed my personal mission statement: *Be as kind as you can possibly be. Inspire compassion in others.* These two sentences have often helped me resist the temptation to become angry, brought me back on track when I have become defensive, helped me have patience with my children, and led me to be of service to others. There is nothing dazzling about my mission statement, any more than there is about a keel hidden beneath a boat that provides stability in turbulent seas. Nonetheless, my mission statement has helped me enormously in keeping my life directed.

Having a mission statement for your life is a quick and essential way to bring your existence into focus and give you purpose. Develop one today. Write it down on several index cards and put them places where you will see them often. For a while, attempt to remind yourself every hour of what your mission statement is.

> *Some people don't know where they want to go but complain a lot about not getting there. Decide* not *to be one of them.*

2

Health is inner peace. Healing is letting go of fear.

Fears hate more than anything else to be defeated. They will try to invade your new truth like a virus, telling you what you can't do, not what you can do, telling you what you can't be, not what you are . . . Don't listen.

—Suze Orman,
in *The 9 Steps to Financial Freedom*

There is more to life than increasing its speed.

—Gandhi

Attitudinal Healing defines health as inner peace, and recognizes that healing is letting go of fear-based thoughts. This definition acknowledges that health and healing are of the mind, and are not based on the condition of your body, your bank account, or your job. Mother Teresa—who worked with starvation, death, and dying—once commented that there was more spiritual deprivation on the streets of New York than on the streets of Calcutta. This statement acknowledges that one can have a youthful, attractive, strong body, a nice suit, and a cell phone and be far from healthy. In short, health and healing are a result of what thoughts you hold in your mind.

There is a very logical progression in this definition:

> If you want to be healthy, devote yourself
> to peace of mind.

> The way you do this is by becoming aware
> of what thoughts are fear-based and then
> letting them go.

When I was in college, a popular bar offered me a job as a bouncer. My job description was straightforward: Determine at the door who was "appropriate" for entrance into the bar and who was not. (At the time my friends said having me as a bouncer was like having the rooster guard the henhouse.) When I made a mistake and let in a "troublemaker," it was then my task to tactfully, and without incident remove the troublemaker from the establishment.

Similarly, it is important to be able to determine what thoughts to let into your mind, and which to keep out. Think of your mind as an "establishment" that is committed to peace of mind. Develop a watchful part of your mind to be a "bouncer" at the door who has the sole purpose of determining whether a certain perception, thought, or belief is conducive to your peace of mind. If it is, gladly let it in. If not, send it on its way. Of course, there is the chance that your bouncer will make a mistake. In this case it is necessary to tactfully, and without incident, remove the "trouble-making thought" from your mind.

Unfortunately, your ego (i.e., the fearful part of yourself that believes you are separate from God) has its own type of bouncer. This bouncer tells you it will keep you safe, but it does so by holding onto thoughts of resentment, hatred, guilt, and fear. It tries to sell you on its insane view of safety by telling you things like:

"Getting even will make you feel better."

"Beat yourself up for your mistakes and you won't repeat them."

"Stay angry with, or even hate, those who

have done you wrong and you will find
security."

What the ego is really concerned with is keeping your
true nature, love, hidden from your awareness.

Create a positive bouncer for your mind. You will
become healthy as you take charge of your own thoughts.
If ever you find yourself with resentful, guilty, or excessively
angry thoughts do the following:

Ask yourself: "Will these thoughts lead me
to have peace of mind?"

Clearly say, "I am devoted to health and
these thoughts are unhealthy."

*When you see the relationship
between your thoughts and your
experience in life you have taken the
largest step toward health.*

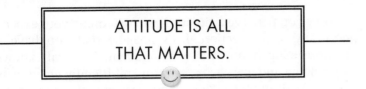

ATTITUDE IS ALL
THAT MATTERS.

Have you ever noticed that two people can confront the same circumstances with very different reactions? This is a matter of attitude and nothing else. Freedom is being able to say, "Rich or poor, alone or with a mate, physically healthy or not, employed or laid off, I believe that peace of mind is possible."

We have all experienced what it is like to be having a perfectly fine day and have a situation or crisis arise that sends us into a tailspin. It may be something small like a traffic jam making us late, or something more severe like the loss of a job. Our response can seem automatic.

Though at first it may be difficult to accept, freedom depends on recognizing that you're not upset because of what occurred, you are upset because of *how you perceive the situation*. Key to Attitudinal Healing is recognizing that you are not a victim of the world.

Another way of saying this is: *There is absolutely nothing in the world that has the power to ruin your day.* If you are upset, it is because *you* have directed your mind to be so. Initially these truths can be hard to accept because you have become so accustomed to giving your power away. Every time you blame another person for your unhappiness you are giving your power away. Stop blaming and start healing.

How you perceive a situation will determine your experience and your reaction. Let's imagine that you have a favorite coffeehouse that you frequent. The staff knows your name and always has a warm and friendly greeting as you walk through the door. An extremely grumpy woman whom you have never seen before serves you this particular morning. She appears preoccupied rather than caring about you or what she is doing. As she pours your hot coffee a good portion spills in your lap. Despite your jumping in shock, no apology follows. Your experience is anger: both toward the waitress and the owner, Joe, for hiring such an incompetent person. Then, a friend of yours at the next booth says, "Isn't it great that Joe hired her!"

"Great! Are you out of your mind? She just spilled hot coffee in my lap and walked away," you reply with your best indignant voice.

"Oh, you didn't hear the story?" your friend whispers.

"What story?" you angrily reply, still drying off your new slacks, wondering how you will go through the day looking as though you wet your pants.

"Yeah, Joe didn't know her from Adam. He read in the paper that her husband had died last month in a car accident. Apparently her husband's health insurance stopped, and she was looking for another job in order to pay for her sixteen-year old son's chemotherapy for leukemia," your friend responds.

Now, you still have hot coffee in your crotch, but are you still angry? Unlikely. The only thing that shifted was your perception and attitude. Through discovering a reason to be compassionate, your entire experience changed—and there are *always* reasons to be compassionate.

An important part of healing (i.e., letting go of fear) is developing compassion. Instead of going out in the world and finding plenty of reasons to be upset, go out and discover reasons to extend love. There are thousands of reasons waiting for you right now. A helpful thought to remember is that a miracle is nothing more than allowing an old grievance to become a current compassion.

If you ever run short on reasons to be compassionate, remember there is always one good reason: It makes you feel better than anything else you could do.

When you are upset remind yourself the cause of your discomfort is your own attitude. This is freedom.

THE WISDOM OF THE
CHINESE FINGER PUZZLE.

In some novelty stores you will find Chinese finger puzzles, small and colorful woven sheaths whose ends you insert both index fingers into. To free yourself, your first reaction is most likely to pull them out. As you may have experienced, this will only tighten the sheath around your fingers.

This is exactly what painful states of mind are like. If you try to get away from past pain, current problems, or an anticipated difficult future by running away or avoiding, the suffering has a way of getting a tighter grip on your life.

The way out of the Chinese finger puzzle offers us four steps that are applicable to our daily life:

1. Be careful not to over-react.

2. Relax and breathe deeply.

3. Move with thoughtful intention and awareness.

4. Once free, only do it again if you really need the practice.

Being careful not to overreact means that you become less controlled by your automatic responses. In order not to have an automatic response, it is important to react to what *is* happening *now,* not what *was* happening *then* (five minutes, five days, or five years ago), or what *might be* happening later.

To have inner peace, become an *Is-Now Person* in your reactions, not a *Was-Then Person* or a *Might-Be Person*. Is-Now's have a lot more fun and joy than Was-Then's or Might-Be's. Is-Now's are also much more efficient and productive because they are dealing with what is, not what was or might be. If you are dealing with what is, you will find it easier to respond with kindness, which creates solutions. If you are coming from what was or what might be, you will probably be operating from fear, and you can end up creating problem after problem.

The most important tool in becoming an Is-Now is to direct your mind to relax, and your breath to deepen. Learn, where applicable, to have at least a 30 second pause between what is happening and your reaction to it. Ask yourself, "Do I want to respond with tension, anxiety, and fear from what was, or with love, compassion, and understanding to what is?"

You have probably noticed that sometimes you can solve a particular problem or situation, only to find yourself in the same or similar circumstances again. You may feel that this is a result of what is happening in the world, not what is happening in your mind. Look again. Once you take your fingers out of the puzzle, don't put them back in unless you want to. Many people will say, "Well, the problem just presented itself again and I had to take care of it." Don't go along with that thinking any longer. Many of your problems in life are because *you agree to participate in them.*

Problems are like dance partners: When they tap you on the shoulder to cut in on your peace of mind, be discerning. Learn to say no to some of your problems and you will have a more peaceful life.

Don't automatically react. If you feel your life tightening around you, pause. Direct your mind and actions in the direction you choose.

IT IS NEVER TOO LATE
TO HAVE A HAPPY CHILDHOOD.

A few months ago I was in a parking lot when a man approached me and said, "Hey, I know you." My ego had a moment of satisfaction for being recognized from my books, or perhaps a lecture. Then the man said, "You're the guy who was with the clown in the circus last night!" In fact, I was. The night before, while with my children attending the circus, I had been chosen by the clown to come into the center ring. After a moment of embarrassment I became quite the ham, and had a great time.

I suppose being remembered as a clown's assistant, rather than an author and psychologist, isn't such a bad thing.

Being an adult can be serious business. Deadlines to meet, bills to pay, problems to solve, and very little time to play. There's a better way.

If you look into the eyes of most spiritual masters you will see incredible depth, peace, and knowledge, but also a playful happy innocence. You cannot be in their presence for long without realizing that a happy child lives within their being. It is through their devotion to a higher power that they feel blessed and loved, and this in turn allows them to be safe, happy, and playful.

This process is available to all of us. A happy childhood, even if you are ninety-two, begins with realizing that God loves you right now and always. God is not all serious business. He wishes happiness for His children. He rejoices when we are light and joyful.

Take time to play. Bring a light-heartedness to your adult activities. The other day, when I was volunteering in my daughter's fourth grade class, I saw a boy making a structure on his desk with his books. I knew this boy to be academically excellent, and did not worry about him playing instead of getting down to business. He was not procrastinating; he was simply having fun. Shortly after witnessing this, I returned home knowing I had bills to pay, an activity that I often dread. I decided to learn from my young friend. Before paying the stack of invoices, I built a structure with the various size envelopes, coloring and decorating them along the way with my kid's art supplies. I imagined the person in the billing department opening an endless sea of envelopes and coming across mine and smiling. It made me feel good. I was having fun with my bills, and maybe even brought a smile to someone else's day!

Most adults dread going to the dentist. I became amazed that my daughters, after a few visits to Dr. Bayless, would actually ask when they could go again. Even after a difficult procedure they still wanted to go back. This is because their dentist makes it fun, and he obviously loves what he does. From my daughters and Dr. Bayless I am reminded that *if you make something playful, and are coming from love, even painful situations will be a positive experience.* Imagine that, actually liking to go to the dentist because it's fun.

Not many people play when they are afraid, angry, or

depressed. Yet, as many cancer researchers have demonstrated, humor and laughter is one way to bring you healing (out of fear) and to health (peace of mind). Most people have peace of mind when they are playing. Heal yourself by playing more.

*Happy playfulness is as much a part
of a spiritual path as is serious prayer.*

This one belief paves the road to success. Despite this, it is not always comfortable to accept, because good excuses are not easily relinquished, especially if you have come to believe that they are true.

You may be reluctant to take full responsibility for your happiness. It is much more convenient and appears easier to place the responsibility for your happiness on something or someone else.

Ask yourself, "What do I need—that I don't have—in order to have peace of mind right now?" Whatever you may come up with—more money, a mate, a better house—*you* have created as a "need for happiness." It is only because you believe that you need these things to be happy that gives them any value. Because of how the ego works, it is likely that even if you had them all you would find other things to need. Until you make the decision to believe that the only limitations to your happiness are the ones you make up, you will never know freedom.

Perhaps you are currently in a difficult situation. You may believe that your present circumstances need to end before you can have happiness and peace. Reexamine this belief.

Even through traumatic situations you can still have peace of mind. People first used Attitudinal Healing to deal with life-threatening disease. Through practicing these principles thousands of people have been able to find peace of mind during the most challenging of times—times that they first thought were their worst nightmare.

Situations arise that can be difficult to not see as limitations on your happiness. The second principle of Attitudinal Healing helps teach that these difficult circumstances are limiting to your peace of mind only to the extent that you allow them to be. You cannot control many things that happen, but you can control how you react to them. Most of these challenging circumstances usually fall into one of three categories: money-, relationship-, or body-related.

Of the three challenges, the largest for me has been a physical disability. I have a severe hearing loss in both ears that has progressively become worse. At this time I have very little of my hearing left. At the initial diagnosis, I believed that my ears were to me, as a psychologist, what hands are to a concert pianist. I went through a period of being very fearful, believing that if I were deaf it was going to be extremely difficult to be happy. I had a physical disability, but it was my thoughts that were placing the limitation on my happiness.

I also have tinnitus, a periodic ringing in the ears. At first this was as bothersome as the hearing loss itself. When my ears would ring it was difficult to concentrate and was a reminder of my progressive deafness. One day, while hiking with a new friend, we had the following conversation:

"I heard about a small culture in South America where the highest of honors is to have ringing in the ears," my friend stated.

"How could such an annoyance be an honor?" I questioned.

"Because to them, the ringing in the ears is a constant reminder to think of God. Those with ringing are seen as blessed," my friend replied.

This was indeed a miracle for me because with three sentences of conversation, what I had placed upon myself as a limitation had been transformed to a gift.

Through the last several years of being severely hearing impaired I have discovered that the limitations of my body don't have to place limitations on my happiness. I have been pleased to learn that there are far more ways to hear than simply through understanding words. Think of hearing as a sponge with many pores. To use only the ears is to use only one pore of the sponge. I am now more aware of hearing with other pores, such as the "ear of the heart." I pay more attention to the "sounds" of love, pain, joy, and despair that lie beneath and beyond the content of words. I honor the internal voice of my intuition more than I used to. The only limitations my hearing loss places upon me are ones that I invent. I am choosing to look for the lessons to be learned rather than the limitations to be invented.

There is a specific vocabulary devoted to limiting your ability to experience love and creativity by reinforcing your belief in reasons not to be happy. These words can be seen as the mortar that holds the bricks of excuses together in your life. If you remove the mortar (the language) the bricks (limitations) are more easily removed. The following are some examples of limiting language used in my book *Healing the Addictive Mind:*

> I *doubt* I could succeed. I know that I
> *should* do it, *but* it is too *difficult.* Besides,
> nobody else seems to be able to succeed; it
> is *impossible.* And I've *tried* it before; I *can't*
> do it. *If only* things were different. I *ought*
> to do it, but I have this *limitation* that
> prevents me.

In addition to the italicized words, any phrases used for categorizing, evaluating, or negatively judging yourself or others will limit your peace of mind. With conscious effort you can eliminate these words from your vocabulary. Richard Bach, in his book *Illusions,* summarizes this aspect of Attitudinal Healing: "Argue for your limitations and sure enough, they're yours."

> *A miracle is nothing more than*
> *being able to let go of a limitation for*
> *happiness and in its place see a gift.*

IF YOU HAVE CONFLICTING GOALS, CONFLICT IS WHAT YOU'LL GET.

If you were asked if you want to be happy, no doubt you would say yes. Few hands go up when asked, "How many people want to suffer today?" Yet, if your happiness is a goal that you haven't become completely committed to, suffering is very likely.

You may still have many other goals that get in the way of your happiness. You also may see some value in not being happy. For example, in some of my lectures I have asked, "How many people would like to be happy all of the time?" Usually only about half the audience raises their hands. When asked why, the answer is that without a little pain, happiness would not be so great. The belief is that you have to know sour to know sweet, suffering to know joy. This is your ego's way of making you keep seeing value in pain. See through this madness. The power of God's Love does not need an opposite to be profoundly experienced.

Peace and happiness are an ancient memory in you that comes forth when your mind is quiet. When your mind is in conflict it is not quiet and therefore cannot remember. Your mind is in conflict whenever you have goals that are based on fear. The following are examples of goals that will lead you to conflict and get in the way of your peace of mind:

CONFLICT CREATING GOALS

I want revenge for what you did to me.

I want you to feel guilty.

I want to hurt you.

I (or you) deserve to suffer.

I want to always be right.

I don't want my body to ever grow old.

I don't want my body to ever die.

I don't want to forgive you.

I want to always please you.

I want my pain to be your fault.

I want to be more important than you are (or vice versa).

I never want to make another mistake.

Removing these goals from your mind is like raising a curtain and discovering love, compassion, and peace waiting patiently behind it. As you decide to see how insane your fear-based goals are, you will not value them any longer. Work on catching yourself when you fall back into fear and ask yourself, "Is what I am thinking *right now* going to give me peace of mind *right now*?"

(*Side with your happiness. More than anything else, focusing on the immediate effects of your thinking will help you heal.*)

LEARN TO SAY "BYE-BYE," "ALL GONE," AND "WHOOPSIE."

When my daughters were toddlers I loved their spontaneity and joy. They had something that I had lost long ago. Observing and playing with them, I learned that their limited language held a great deal of wisdom.

Try simplifying your life and increasing your peace of mind by practicing three pieces of Toddler Wisdom:

Bye-Bye Wisdom:

Part of growing up is learning the delicate balance of being dependent and independent. Toddlers can go through some separation anxiety, but ultimately and ideally, they learn that they are loved and cared for. With this they are able to say "bye-bye" and know they are not being left. The same is now true with your relationship with God. You may have conflict and anxiety in your life because you have been away from your spirituality for so long that you believe you are all alone. This makes it difficult to let go, even when it is time to move on. Developing your spirituality will allow you to feel more completely loved and cared for, and will help you let go of circumstances, people, and material possessions that are no longer in your best interest. When you take in that God has never left you; you will more easily be able to let go of situations when the time has come.

All-Gone Wisdom:

When toddlers finishes a yummy meal they may look down and say, "All gone!" There is joy and an innocent kind of gratitude in their expression. They are ready to receive whatever is next. As adults we can believe that more is better, or become far too concerned with not having enough of something (money, love, material possessions). We can forget the "all-gone wisdom" which knows that when something is over, a space for something new can be created. Joyful anticipation beats dreaded worry, don't you think?

When I was in third-world countries I would see children joyfully playing on dirt floors with toys made from discarded items. They teach us: Be joyous with what you have, and don't make the mistake of thinking that more will make you happier.

At the end of each day say, "All gone," and be ready to receive the next experience in your life. You will find that this process of staying open will bring much more prosperity to your life than worrying about not having enough or losing what you have.

Whoopsie Wisdom:

Given a loving environment, when a toddler makes a mistake they don't make a big deal out of it. Their response is usually something like, "Whoopsie." Once you begin to realize that God loves you no matter what, you will be more able to take mistakes in stride. The knowledge that you are loved provides tremendous freedom to grow. The next time you make a mistake and are tempted to be hard on yourself, instead say, "Whoopsie," and don't allow your mistake to weigh you down.

Toddler Wisdom:
Say, "Bye-bye," and have joyful anticipation.
Say, "All gone," and be ready to receive.
Say, "Whoopsie," and move on.

3

Giving and receiving are the same.

> *When I was in London, I went to see the home-less people where our sisters have a soup kitchen. One man, who was living in a cardboard box, held my hand and said, "It's been a long time since I felt the warmth of a human hand."*
>
> Mother Teresa, in *A Simple Path*

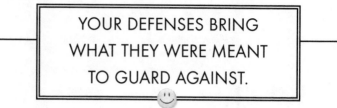

YOUR DEFENSES BRING WHAT THEY WERE MEANT TO GUARD AGAINST.

There is a wonderful little piece of magic that you can discover anytime, anywhere: When you give unconditional love, you will receive it— magnified and with no delay. The great thing about this principle is that it is so easily tested, and nothing is required of you that you don't already possess.

Attitudinal Healing teaches that it is through giving and receiving which you will discover health and happiness. It also recognizes a basic spiritual truth: Giving and receiving are the same. The largest obstacle to giving and receiving is the fearful voice inside of you that makes statements such as, "If I give I will just be taken advantage of again." Or, "If I give, you'd better be grateful and do something nice for me in return." These are your defenses. You created them because you want love and don't want to be hurt. The problem is your defenses keep love from you and bring pain to your life.

Defenses are ways of thinking and acting which you believe will protect you from being hurt. Yet in actuality, your defenses will ultimately bring what they were meant to guard against.

Have you ever known somebody who dreams of having a great relationship, but believes that nobody can be trusted and therefore treats everyone with a good deal of distrust? Not surprisingly they don't find someone to love and trust fully—few want to stick around while being treated like they can't be trusted. Or, have you known people who have had a very painful past, and as a result, put tremendous defensive energy into not letting something similar happen again? They usually end up alone or with someone who repeats the pattern of their pain. For example, most adults who grew up in an alcoholic family swear that the same havoc will not be in their lives again. And yet, without awareness, their defenses will often bring them what they were meant to guard against: They either marry a chemically dependent person or become one themselves.

Your defenses can be hard to get rid of because you may have strong, even seemingly logical, arguments for why you need them. Try a little experiment. *Instead of being afraid of not getting what you want, give what it is that you do want.* This creates a force in your life that will make your dreams come true and your defenses melt away. Remember, in giving do not focus on the other person's reaction. Rather, place your awareness on the universal law that you receive what you give.

*Your defenses are dams
that block miracles from
flowing naturally in your life.*

FOR ONE WEEK, GO OUT OF YOUR WAY TO GIVE . . . CHEERFULLY.

Another person's requests for a loving response from you may come in many forms. Not all of them are pretty and some may make you very uncomfortable. I have worked with adolescents who were so angry and void of love that they threatened my life. Yet love is what they needed and were requesting.

Even when somebody you care deeply about requests a loving response, you may be tempted to come up with many reasons why you can't, don't want to, or shouldn't involve yourself. Maybe you think they deserve your anger more than your love because of something they did.

Most of the reasons to withhold love are based on the fearful voice in your mind that keeps score. "Let's see, I have done nice things for you for three nights, now you have to do something for me." This type of conditional giving is little more than a business transaction, and has nothing to do with expanding your happiness. True giving is not a tidy business transaction where you give with the expectation of something in return from the person.

The ego's law is: When you do something for someone else, be damn sure you get something back. If you don't, stop giving.

Attitudinal Healing recognizes the law of love: Give love unconditionally and your life will be transformed.

Acting from love will open doors you never imagined were there, as the following story illustrates. When I asked the director of the Austin Center for Attitudinal Healing, Doug Mullins, how he ended up doing the work he was doing he said, "I was living in Colorado, making a fantastic living in computers. I had moved from Texas many years previously. I loved Colorado, and had vowed when I left Texas that I would not return. Colorado was exactly where I wanted to be. Then my daughter, who I had not always had the best relationship with, came to me and asked if I would move to Texas so she could finish school there. It was *the last* thing I wanted. But when she asked, something inside of me said I needed to do it. I knew it was the voice of Love. After being in Texas for a while, the Center ended up needing a director. The Center was a hair away from having to close, and stop serving the hundreds of people it had reached. Here I am and I know I am in the right place. If I had not honored my daughters request, I would not be here."

I am not suggesting that one should never say "no." Certainly, having good boundaries is important. However, fear of giving is epidemic in western culture. Generally, people are too focused on what they are going to get from life, rather than what they can give. The result of focusing on "getting" is depression, anger, and isolation, not to mention environmental disaster. Attitudinal Healing guides you to the opportunity to heal through extending love, kindness, and compassion.

In order to experience how giving and receiving are the same, for one week stop focusing on "getting." Stop making sure that you get your share back. Stop worrying about what you will miss or lose if you give freely. For one week respond to everything you can with love. Give some of your time. Offer acceptance and understanding. Listen to people. This type of service will teach you that giving and receiving are the same.

Unconditional love wants to give itself freely. Fear-based giving always wants a return on the investment.

CHOOSE AN HOUR A WEEK TO REACH OUT.

"I don't have time." This is a common response to why one can't be giving in the community. It's no wonder. In the United States today people work longer hours and commute longer distances than ever before. Many people still make charitable contributions with their money, which is wonderful, but few actively give of their time. Imagine the world if everyone devoted just one hour a week to doing acts of kindness.

There is simple wisdom in the saying, "Practice random acts of kindness and senseless acts of beauty."

It doesn't matter where you start extending love. It only matters that you see it as much of a priority as all of your other activities. If you spend some time each week giving unconditionally, you will find all other areas of your life uplifted. When you take the time out of your stressful life to give, your whole life becomes less stressful and more purposeful. You are also to likely find the attitude of unconditional giving spreading over to your other activities, bringing increased peace and calm to your life.

Some people find it helpful to have structure to their giving: Volunteering with an organization, school, retirement home, hospital, or the like. Other people like the adventure of setting out for an hour each week to find someone to give to: Perhaps a neighbor doing yard work, a homeless person on a bench, an abandoned animal. It matters little who the recipient is, it is the act of compassion that will heal your life and contribute to the healing the world.

I had a friend, Max, who died a few years back—well into his nineties. For over fifty years he walked Carmel Beach every morning, picking up garbage. I think he lived so long and with such joy because of those morning walks of service to nature.

It is easy to become hopeless and overwhelmed by all the problems and atrocities in the world. Train your mind to know that extending love makes a difference. Don't just sit and read the newspaper, wondering what is happening to the world. Make a difference by taking an hour a week to make happy news. At the end of the week, if one life on the planet, or the planet itself, feels a little more cared about because of your decision to take the time to give, you have made an invaluable contribution.

Acts of love are what will bring peace to your life and to the world.

SMILE GENTLY
AND OFTEN.

Not much is needed to smile—just a glimpse of who you really are. The wonderful thing is that it works in reverse, too. If you consistently take the time to smile softly and gently, and give yourself a few moments of silence, you experience who you are: a being created in God's Love.

The magic of a smile doesn't stop here. When another person sees you smile from knowing who you are, it touches something in them. Smiles are contagious, and it is okay to infect as many people as you can.

Smiling with compassion is the simplest of ways to experience giving and receiving are the same. It is impossible to share such a smile and not feel your heart be uplifted. If you smile because you see the beauty in another person, or in nature, you begin to feel beautiful yourself. Try these smile exercises and experience immediate results.

- Find a quiet place to sit and set aside five
  minutes. Close your eyes and deepen your
  breathing. Purposefully smile gently—a
  barely noticeable smile. Keep breathing
  slow deep breaths, and keep smiling. You
  may want to do this with no words, or you
  can try saying to yourself several times, "I

am created in love." Welcome the feelings that come and experience your smile as it extends through your entire being.

- Take time to smile at people today. Don't wait for something good to happen. Smile because there is joy in you wanting to express itself. Even if you are not aware of this joy, it is there, and your smile will be the window through which it can enter your awareness. Just as you would open a window to let fresh air into a stuffy room, smile to let joy into an upset mind. Noticing how your smile affects other people will also make it worth your while.

Some people might say, "Well, I don't have anything to smile about. Look at my life. It's horrible." Your life may be the way it is because you are too focused upon your misfortune. If you don't believe you have anything to smile about, you won't. Alternatively, as you realize you always have something to smile about your life will change. It may seem paradoxical, but *smile so you will have something to smile about.*

*Smile for no good reason and you
will discover the best reason to smile:
Joy and peace live in you always.*

THOSE WHO
GIVE, HAVE.

Happiness is an equal opportunity experience. Despite what you may believe, happiness has nothing to do with race, socio-economic status, physical condition, or intelligence. There is a simple rule of thumb for happiness and love: Those who give, have.

During one of my internships with mentally challenged kids and adults I found it a bit amusing that the "patients" seemed to be much more joyful than the staff treating them. These happy souls became my teachers. In them I saw a constant demonstration of giving love. When someone was sad, an embrace and a kind word were always given. When someone needed assistance it was always offered, with no thought of reciprocation. Rarely did I witness resentment because of everyday inconveniences, jealousies, or a larger life crisis. When conflict did arise, they did not come up with a whole lot of reasons to hold grudges. They rarely wanted to punish and most always wanted to forgive with a big hug and simple heartfelt words. During the Special Olympics I saw no pettiness, only mutual support and unbelievable enthusiasm. In short, these remarkable individuals taught me that being happy is a direct result of not focusing on the past and future. They demonstrated the power of giving and receiving love in the present moment.

Don't worry, no one needs to lower their IQ 20 points to be happy. The ability to think and be creative is a remarkable gift. But the undisciplined mind can turn on itself, creating suffering while promising it is saving you. Attitudinal Healing helps us to direct our mind toward giving unconditionally, clearing the way to receive more than we ever imagined.

When you hold onto past resentments you hurt yourself. When you offer compassion and understanding you heal yourself. This law never changes.

ARE YOU GIVING WHAT YOU WANT FOR YOURSELF?

There are many myths about happiness. Most of them are based on the belief that if you are not feeling happy it's because you have not found the right place to live, the right job, or the right mate.

There are essentially three ways your mind will tell you to achieve happiness. They are named for their central characteristic. Only one of them will work, but the good news is that it is never too late to change.

Panhandling:

This way of thinking says, "Your heart is empty, so sit and wait for some 'spare love' to come your way." Those in this pattern of thinking tend to come from a background where they either have not had much support or have been heavily criticized. It is easy for them to live a life where possibilities are never seen, let alone realized. Because they are afraid to love, they wait with their hand outstretched for something in life to be given to them by people they perceive as having more. They tend to feel that the world happens to them and they are just along for the ride. If things are going well, they consider themselves lucky. If things are going bad, they feel like a victim, blaming other people, circumstances, or God.

Seeking and Chasing:

This way of thinking says, "Your heart is empty, but there is so much out there that could fill it. Go get some." Here the emphasis is upon looking for something or someone to make you happy. These individuals may have taken the essential step of asking themselves what they want, and may appear active and assertive in creating what they want, but they end up disillusioned time and time again. They are encouraged by a culture which believes the same thing they do, so it is difficult for them to see the insanity. At most they have fleeting periods of happiness because if they experience suffering they always look to something else on the horizon—a habit which is precisely the cause of the suffering.

Giving and Receiving:

This way of thinking says, "God's Love is in you now. To know it, give it," reflecting the universal truth that giving and receiving are the same. These individuals have not only asked themselves what they want, they have also recognized that what brings happiness, Love, can only increase by giving it away. This takes the focus off of material accumulation and external recognition and onto such traits as love, understanding, patience, tolerance, gentleness, and compassion. This way of thinking knows there is nothing constructive in sitting and lamenting about not having what you want. Give what you want for yourself and receive the same.

Suze Orman, in her book *The 9 Steps to Financial Freedom,* shares the following experiment: Clench your fists tightly shut, as though you were holding onto something you were afraid you were going to lose. Feel the tension this creates, and how difficult it would be to receive something, even if it were handed directly to you. Now, have relaxed hands; palms open and outstretched, as though you were about to offer somebody something. Can you not receive more easily when you are also in the position of giving?

In actuality there are five steps you can follow to increase your happiness.

1. Identify the ways you have believed you would achieve happiness.

2. With honesty and clarity, decide if these beliefs are accurate.

3. If they are not, determine to let go of them.

4. Decide what really will result in your happiness.

5. Start doing this.

These steps sound almost too simple to even bother saying. Yet many people keep doing the same things even though happiness never comes. Practicing Attitudinal Healing can help you stop creating suffering for yourself when you think you are striving for happiness.

The only productive use of time
is to give what you truly want for yourself.

4

We can let go of the past and of the future.

Another word for quiet is "now."

Hugh Prather,
in *Notes on How to Live in
this World . . . and Still be Happy.*

You have likely heard the importance of setting and achieving goals countless times. For right now, forget about it. Setting goals for the future may be important, but it is nowhere near as important as learning to be present.

Sometimes the real go-getters become anxious at the suggestion of letting go of goals, even for a moment. Don't worry, future-oriented goals are certainly not all negative. Yet if they are your whole life and you always go from one goal to the next, you are not going to find consistent happiness.

By now you are seeing that focusing on the moment is a central point of Attitudinal Healing. Without it, your happiness will always be fleeting. To get an idea of where you stand in being present, get out a piece of paper and divide it into three columns; past, now, and future. Contemplate your life and what you spend your time thinking about. Then place in the three columns the percentage of time that you spend in each. If you are like most people you will discover that you spend far more time holding onto grudges or guilt about the past, and worrying or trying to control the future, than you do living in the present. With awareness and intention this can change.

On this morning's news I saw a physician/mountaineer who was caught in a severe storm a few years ago on Mount

Everest. Most of his party died. He lost his nose and hands due to frostbite. On the news he was describing how he had been well on his way toward achieving his goal of ascending the great mountain peaks of the world. To his surprise it was through his failure on Everest that he learned his most important lesson. He acknowledged how he had been so goal-oriented that he overlooked his heart, his love for his family, and who he was. Though he lost the hands that had helped him reach his goals, he discovered the heart that delivered him home. "I would never trade them back," he said, his voice trembling with emotion.

To bring a little now to your later, you will need to have strong intentions. This is because your mind is accustomed to obsessing on the past and the future. To break the habit, and bring your mind home to peace, a daily discipline is necessary. If you just leave your mind to go where it will, it will undoubtedly continue to be preoccupied with the past and future, and you will literally put off being happy.

Here is an alternative. In the morning, before your feet hit the floor, establish spiritually-based goals *that can be accomplished in the moment throughout the day*. These goals will bring balance to your life and any future-oriented goals you may have. Examples of these peace-ensuring goals are:

My goal is to listen with my heart today.

My goal is to extend kindness to all I meet.

My goal is to forgive rather than judge.

My goal is to give Love.

The following is a five-step meditation you can do each day to focus on creating peace-ensuring goals. I suggest you practice it each morning when you wake. It is easy to remember because it is an acronym for PEACE. Thus I call it the PEACE Plan.

Picture how you want to feel today and the thoughts you want to have in your mind.

Notice I didn't say "what you want to have happen," for this is often out of your control. But what you think and feel *in reaction to* external circumstances is completely up to you. This may be hard to see right now, but it is true. It is also the key to your happiness.

Expect that you will think these thoughts and feel this way.

This step uproots the common habit of saying, *"Yeah, but* if something happens that I don't like, I will have every reason to be angry and upset." Today escape this pattern of giving up your happiness by knowing that *you alone* choose your thoughts and feelings.

Ask, "What is my peace-ensuring goal for the day?"

Peace-ensuring goals are ones that can be accomplished in the moment and result in you being peaceful and happy.

*Choose to listen to the gentle voice
within you as it offers you your answer.*

*Enjoy your day and share your peace-ensuring
goal with at least one other person.*

*By practicing peace-ensuring goals
you will add a little now to your
later, and a smile to your life.*

It seems that in today's world everybody wants more energy. Millions use caffeine, even amphetamines and cocaine. News of the latest food, supplement, or exercise that increases energy fill the tabloids.

If you want real and complete energy all you need to learn about is love.

In 1981 I spent a few days traveling across India by car with Mother Teresa, stopping in many locations each day. There was not much time for rest other than a brief nod-off in the back seat (please, no jokes about sleeping with Mother Teresa). The schedule was fast paced, and the conditions of poverty we entered were often extremely difficult. At the time I was in my twenties and an athlete. She was more than three times my age, and in failing health. I was the one exhausted. Later I realized this was because my response to the poverty and illness I saw was to be overwhelmed and to fear that the relief of suffering of so many was hopeless. Her response was one of compassion and deep love. I believe this was the source of her endless energy.

Most people have absolutely no idea how much energy their fear consumes. Like persistent erosion, your fears eat away at your life even when you're not thinking directly about them—even in your sleep. Eventually you may not even notice what a state of stress and anxiety you are in because you forget what peace feels like. If you are not careful, fear becomes that which motivates you. Fear-based motivation never results in peace.

Most fear comes from projecting a negative past into the future. The good news is that it's possible to let go of the past and the future, and thus experience a renewed sense of energy. The following exercise will help you start.

Write down your three biggest fears—the ones that you rarely, if ever, talk about. Fears like, "I am afraid I will be discovered to be incompetent," or, "I am afraid I will be alone all my life," or "I am afraid to die." Read these aloud to yourself and then say, "My mind made these up. Instead of focusing on these fears, I can choose to love." Next, spend five minutes extending love to the part of you that is so fearful. For example, say to the fear of incompetence, "No matter what mistakes you make, you are loved." To the fear of being alone, say, "God's Love is available for you to give and receive right now. You are not alone." To the fear of death, say, "Love is eternal. You have nothing to fear."

The best way to get through your fears is to recognize that the solution is always to love. Practicing this with your fears will give you more and lasting energy than even the best double espresso.

The greatest energy depleter is your fear.
The most powerful energizer is love.

Quicksand. Just the word conjures up images of an old Tarzan movie: a naive visitor to the jungle takes that fateful step into the pit of sludge, thinking it solid ground. In some scenes, all that was left of the poor traveler was a safari hat resting on the surface. As a kid I watched enough Tarzan movies to learn that the thing to do if you step into quicksand is be still and hope somebody throws you a nearby vine.

Quicksand Thinking. As the term suggests, this is when you step into a disguised and dangerous thought system and begin to sink faster than the poor fellow in the Tarzan movie. Unless you are still and grab a vine, soon all that will remain is your hat floating on the surface.

The most common form of Quicksand Thinking is *When-Then* and *If-Then* beliefs. When you engage in If-Then thinking, you believe peace of mind is impossible because of something that occurred in the past. When you engage in When-Then thinking you believe that your happiness is conditional upon something happening in the future.

The first step in getting out of Quicksand Thinking is knowing you are in it. This entails identifying your If-Then and When-Then thinking. We all have our favorites, but the following is a list of common If-Then and When-Then statements. If yours are not included, feel free to add to the list.

FAVORITE IF-THEN BELIEFS

If I had slept better last night, *then* I could be more pleasant.

If you had not done what you did, *then* I could be happy.

If I'd had a better childhood, *then* I could be happy.

If I had been born with a different body, *then* I would be happier.

If I hadn't married you, *then* I would be happy.

FAVORITE WHEN-THEN BELIEFS

When you apologize, *then* I will forgive you.

When I have more money, *then* I will be happier.

When I lose some weight, *then* I will like myself.

When I am no longer ill, *then* I will be happy.

When I find the right partner, *then* I will be happy.

In the Tarzan movies, if the unfortunate soul in the quicksand was smart enough to know he was in quicksand and stay still, the next step was to hope somebody would throw him a vine. In your life, that somebody is God, and He has plenty of vines to toss you. It is possible that you have just let the vine sit there while you sank in Quicksand Thinking. Be sure not to do this anymore. When you know you are in Quicksand Thinking, be still. Then ask for help from God. Asking for help is really no big deal or fancy prayer. All you need to do is say something like, "This way of thinking is hurting me and other people. What would You have me think instead?"

When you feel you are sinking:
Be still. Ask for help. Grab the vine.

BE A BEGINNER.

Anybody who has taken up a sport such as skiing and felt their leg twist in unnatural ways while screaming loudly to the person about to be run over, can attest that it is more impressive to be an expert than a fledging beginner. Yet if you fully allow yourself to be a beginner at something you adopt an attitude that is totally open to learning. However, when you are overly concerned with how you look, or attached to mastering something, you lose a vital part of learning.

Beginner's Mind is a state of being in the present. Instead of investing yourself in being absolutely fantastic at something (attached to the future), or not wanting to look like a complete idiot yet again (reliving the past), you say with joy, "What is there to learn here?"

Many of the best solutions don't come from the "experts." When you have Expert Mind you tend to have a closed system where new information or creative responses are rejected. Beginner's Mind allows you to approach all situations with a fresh mind, creating endless opportunities for creative solutions.

In the late seventies, my father started a program called "Children as Teachers of Peace." Groups of children, from different ethnic backgrounds and cultures met with the world's prominent leaders. The philosophy behind the program was that children can have a simple and fresh look at the world's complicated problems. They recognize love when they see it, and they recognize the need for compassion and understanding when they see it. My daughters have always been very concerned about racism (interestingly, one of them, Jalena, was born at the same time Nelson Mandela was released from prison). Even though Dr. Martin Luther King was deceased, Jalena wanted to share her heart with him, as the following letter reflects:

> *Dear Dr. King:*
>
> *I live in a safe place, and I am happy. I love to hear about you. I think you must be a very loving person. I have some friends like you. They are black and I love them equally as well as all my friends. I bet you were the best friend anybody could have. Is it fun up there?*
>
> *Your friend,*
> *Jalena, age 8*

In all of your endeavors try to have the attitude of being a beginner, even if you are very accomplished. For example, for many years I have been a student of the martial arts. Despite years of practice, if I have the mentality of "I'm an expert black belt" my training is hindered. When I walk onto the mat to practice, I always pause to become a beginner, and see all participants as my teachers, regardless of their background. *If I have something to prove, I won't learn. If I have something to learn, there is nothing to prove.* This is true in all areas of life.

Become a beginner in life. Decide not to be a performer and start being a learner. It's much more fun.

(*With Beginners Mind racism is impossible, withholding love absurd, and listening and wanting to understand come naturally.*)

THROW AWAY YOUR
SCORE CARD.

As much as most people dislike bureaucracy and petty details, it is amazing how much red tape exists in our minds. Sometimes when another person needs your help you might find yourself "reviewing their records" to determine whether you should put yourself out or not. Your internal dialogue might resemble a parole hearing: "One moment, please, while I process your request for release. According to my records, you didn't help me with the dishes last night, you forgot our anniversary two years ago, and you have been more than a little ornery lately. Your overall record is dismal. I am so sorry, your request for kindness and patience is being denied. Try again later when you have improved your score."

Keeping score may make you feel superior, but it will ultimately only lead to bitterness and guilt. Acts of love that are given when somebody has not been a saint are the ones that matter the most. Love and kindness are easy when someone is spreading rose petals in your direction. It's another story when they are spreading manure.

Who hasn't said and done some pretty raunchy stuff? If you ask yourself what you really needed during those times, even though you couldn't say it, was it not love?

When adults or children are acting out in some way, it

isn't beneficial to only be critical. This is the reaction they are used to. If you can find it in yourself to approach them compassionately, knowing that they are in need of love, the situation almost always turns the corner. To help with this, imagine yourself acting like they are. How would you feel? What would you most want? Give this to them now. It will be as healing for you as for them.

None of this is to suggest that people should not be held responsible for their behavior. Consequences are often needed. But, remember it is during the tough times that your compassion is most needed. Throw away your score card and be willing to come from the heart. Regardless if the other person's behavior changes you will find yourself more at peace—and isn't that what it's all about?

If you offer compassion when you receive manure, you will get roses.

DO IT WITH PRESENCE.

There is no such thing as a useless task, only useless thoughts while doing one. No matter what the task is, it holds the opportunity for the experience of complete peace of mind. There is no moment, and no place, where peace cannot enter. It awaits your invitation.

In some of his talks and writings, the Buddhist monk Thich Nhat Hahn offers this meditation:

> Breathing in, I calm my body.
> Breathing out, I smile.
> Dwelling in the present moment
> I know this is a wonderful moment.

Think of all the activities that you do with the goal of getting them over with so you can move on to something more fun or important: Those little necessities like dinner dishes after a long day. In your lifetime you will spend thousands of hours doing these tasks, so why not learn how to make them part of your spiritual growth?

You can hear the difference when music is played with soulful presence. The musician and the listener are moved. The same is true for the way you live your life. When you do something without presence and awareness it is lacking something essential, and you are missing an opportunity for growth. Instead of doing a task to get it over with, do it to become present and joyful. Practice Thich Nhat Hahn's meditation, and add to the third line the task you are doing. For example, you might say:

> *Breathing in, I calm my body.*
> *Breathing out, I smile.*
> *Dwelling in the present moment as I wash this plate,*
> *I know this is a wonderful moment.*

With this type of practice it is possible to have tremendous joy even while doing mundane tasks. Instead of thinking about something else when you drive the car, address envelopes, or walk the dog, bring your full attention to what you are doing. In doing so everyday chores can become growthful activities.

During the course of your day you can bring this same awareness to even the smallest of encounters you have with people. Typically you have many small communications that can mistakenly be seen as insignificant—the clerk at the store, the bank teller, the mail person. During these you may be thinking about other things besides who is in front of you. Instead, make every encounter an opportunity to become present—to offer love. In this context, use Thich Nhat Hahn's meditation by adding to the second and fourth line. For example:

> *Breathing in, I calm my body.*
> *Breathing out, I smile in recognizing you.*
> *Dwelling in the present moment*

I know this is a wonderful moment that I share with you.

You can feel the difference when somebody genuinely meets you. People will also remember your thoughtful presence.

> *Joy does* not *come from what you are doing, but rather from your thoughtful presence while you are doing it. Therefore, any activity can offer joy.*

```
┌─────────────────────────────┐
│  SPEND MORE TIME            │
│  REMEMBERING WHO YOU        │
│  ARE THAN BECOMING          │
│  WHO YOU WANT TO BE.        │
└─────────────────────────────┘
```

You can spend a good deal of time, effort, and resources trying to become the person that you want to be. This pursuit can be a double-edge sword.

There is an inherent problem in approaching yourself with the belief that there is something wrong with or lacking in who you are. Surely, it is admirable to want to become a kinder person, but until you begin to remember that you are as God created you, you will never find lasting peace. When you believe you are something other than love, improving yourself is like blowing up a balloon that has a small leak. You will be able to rise only so far before needing to be "pumped up" again.

In contrast, when you begin to remember the love in which you were created, self-improvement endures because of the solid foundation from which it began. Your relationships become purposeful and more loving.

The core of any spiritual path is simply to remember who you are. Life is not about achieving or acquiring, it is about remembering. *Spiritual remembering requires a willingness to let go of guilt.* The goal of a spiritual path is *not* to beat yourself up for who you think you have been, or to spend all your time hoping to be somebody different in the future. Spirituality focuses on remembering who you are in the eternal moment.

There are many ways to help facilitate spiritual remembering. Most all of them have to do with *doing less* and *paying attention more*. Below are a few examples:

Do less thinking and pay more attention to your heart.

Do less acquiring and pay more attention to what you always have.

Do less complaining and pay more attention to giving.

Do less controlling and pay more attention to letting go.

Do less criticizing and pay more attention to complimenting.

Do less arguing and pay more attention to forgiveness.

Do less high-tech and pay more attention to nature.

Do less running around and pay more attention to stillness.

Do less talking and pay more attention to silence.

Do less hating and pay more attention to common interests.

Do less attacking and pay more attention to the call for love.

Do less obsessing about the past and future and pay more attention to right now.

Do less thinking about what is wrong and pay more attention to what is right.

You don't need to stop any self-improvement you are now doing, but you would do well to spend more time remembering who you are. Each day choose one of the above examples. Practice it, and you will begin to remember who you are.

> *Spiritual remembering comes as you do less from fear and pay more attention to love.*

5

Now is the only time there is, and each instant is for giving.

There is no condition, no circumstance, no problem that love cannot solve . . . love, for yourself and others, is always the solution.

—Neale Donald Walsch,
in *A Friendship with God*

Linus: I guess it's wrong always to be worrying about tomorrow. Maybe we should think only about today.
Charlie Brown: No, that's giving up. I'm still hoping that yesterday will get better.

Charles Schultz, *Peanuts*

HAVE PEACE OF MIND
AS YOUR SINGLE GOAL.

In years past, I would accomplish a goal, have a moment of satisfaction, go on to the next goal, achieve that one, only to repeat the pattern. I became a busy achiever but I wasn't very happy. I had the trappings of success, but the grass was often greener on the other side. Consistent peace of mind eluded me.

Despite being unhappy, I use to think I was successful because I could reach many of the goals that I set. Now it seems crazy to consider myself successful if I am not happy. In fact, I would go so far as to say that the key ingredient to success *is* happiness.

Some goals can be very important, like making enough money for your kid's education, or eating a healthier diet and exercising more. There are many books and seminars on clarifying, setting, and achieving these types of goals. Yet, many of these approaches miss an important point:

> There is only one goal that ultimately matters, one that is an essential part of all others, one that is available to you at all times—*peace of mind.*

Having peace of mind in the present moment as your single goal allows you to pursue any future-oriented objectives with a sense of calm.

When you have peace of mind as your single goal you are saying to yourself: "No matter what is happening in my life—no matter what my physical condition, rich or poor, no matter if people don't behave and react to me how I want them to—peace of mind is most important, and is always possible."

Imagine that your thoughts are like a swinging pendulum. Peace of mind is where the pendulum will naturally come to rest when given a chance. Calmness enters your life when you turn your mind toward peace because there is nothing more powerful than responding to your call home.

A key ingredient to happiness is to realize that now is the only time there is and each instant is for giving.

Most people pay more attention to the contents of their refrigerator and their bank account than they do the content of their mind. Yet, in order to be truly happy we must first take responsibility for our thoughts.

Think of responsibility as the "ability to respond." If you're holding onto thoughts about the past, or are preoccupied with thoughts about the future, you limit your ability to respond to what is happening now.

Don't make the mistake of underestimating the power of your thoughts. Even the smallest pebble dropped into a pond sends ripples in all directions. It is the same with your thoughts. Simply put, your thoughts are the cause of your suffering, and they hold your release.

A different job, more free time, a different relationship, a long vacation, a new purchase: These are common solutions to feeling something is amiss in life. Though these changes can be positive, they do nothing to address the real cause of your conflict: your thoughts. External changes alone are like giving a new paint job to car with engine problems. When you are unhappy, get in the habit of looking at the engine (i.e., your thoughts) instead of the paint (i.e., the external world).

Bumper sticker philosophy points to the superficial ways in which we look for happiness: "When the going gets tough, the tough go shopping." "The one who dies with the most toys wins." These sayings are good examples of believing that more will make you happier. Your experience is transformed when you change your thoughts of desire to thoughts of giving in the moment. If you want real happiness change these sayings to:

"When the going gets tough, the tough give."

"The one who dies having forgiven all is already in Heaven."

Because you may have become accustomed to believing that the external world is the source of your experience, it may initially be difficult to believe that all your thoughts create. For example, it is easy to believe that your emotions are like reflexes and they automatically happen when given certain input from the world. This is not true. The feelings and emotions you experience are your creation.

If you are thinking thoughts that are resentful, are you not creating feelings of anger? If you are thinking thoughts about how unloved you are, are you not creating feelings of loneliness? In contrast, if you are thinking forgiving thoughts, are you not creating feelings of love? If you are directing your mind to think with God, are you not creating feelings of deep connection and joy? To change your life for the better, become aware of your thoughts and decide to become active in directing them toward love and kindness.

Remind yourself often: All thoughts create.
Then decide what it is that you want to make.

Perhaps the most overlooked expression of love is the most powerful: listening. This simple act goes beyond any words that you might say. Sometimes I remind myself of this by saying, "God gave me two ears and one mouth so I could listen twice as much as I talk."

While facilitating groups, I have noticed a common process. When participants are asked to introduce themselves and say a little about their background, listening all but stops. The closer an individual comes to their turn to speak, the less they listen to what is being said. Prior to speaking, they are busy mentally rehearsing what they are going to say. After speaking there is a momentary feeling of relief, and then they begin critiquing their performance. With all of this mental activity, there's little time to listen to what is happening in the present moment.

When you are worrying, rehearsing, criticizing, and judging you are not listening. If you are not listening it is difficult to be loving. Whenever you find yourself in conflict with another person pause and choose to bring your focus back to listening—which is giving—and your experience will change.

My daughters have been excellent teachers to me with regard to the power of listening. Listening to them with interest and lack of judgment clearly builds their self-esteem more than anything I could say. When I do this, I feel on top of the world.

The need to be heard and accepted doesn't change as we become adults. I have a rule of thumb in my communications:

One minute of listening is worth five of talking.

Take time to listen to people with interest, lack of judgment, and understanding. Sometimes, problem solving and advice-giving only get in the way of allowing the person to feel heard. Resist the temptation to always offer advice or constantly try to fix problems, even if you have a perfect solution. Simply listen and empathize without becoming too verbose. Refrain from saying things that begin with words like, "Have you tried . . ." or "I think you should . . ." or "Let me tell you about the time that happened to me. . . ." Whatever follows these words will usually either be trying to solve a problem or taking the focus off of the person and redirecting it onto you. Instead, imagine yourself in their shoes, and then say things like, "I can understand how you would feel that way" (assuming that you do after listening). These responses are validating because the person feels heard.

The next time you think you have the answers for somebody remind yourself:

Listening goes much further to building positive relationships than giving advice ever will.

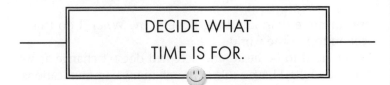

"It takes time." This statement is given vastly more credence than it deserves. Certainly think twice about applying it to your spiritual growth. The truth is that *the spiritual use of time is to give and receive love in this moment.* In this practice, you need not wait for release and freedom.

There are two ways to use time: one is of the ego and the other is of the spirit. Your ego uses time to create a situation where it promises good things in the future yet never lets you feel fully satisfied if and when they arrive. This keeps you always thinking that your ship is about to come in. The emphasis is on hurrying up because time is running out, which creates incredible stress. To the ego, the end of time is death, as is reflected in its motto, "Life's a bitch and then you die."

The higher use of time is devoted to your spiritual development. The focus is on the endless gifts of the present moment—no constant worries, no uninterrupted stress and anxiety, only infinite peace. To understand time in the context of spiritual development is to see that now is the only time there is, and that each instant is for giving. You will do well to let go of the ego's motto and begin to live by love's: "Life is for loving, and love is eternal."

The ego uses a single unrelenting tool to keep you chained to its use of time: guilt. Guilt is the primary obstacle that keeps you from feeling peace. Don't underestimate the extent to which you keep yourself stuck by believing in it.

You get to choose how you want to use time. It is therefore important that you clearly recognize the two choices. They are:

Do you want to use guilt to keep yourself and others in a painful past?

Do you want to use forgiveness to set yourself and others free?

You can use time to beat somebody up, with statements like, "It will be a cold day in Hell before I ever speak to you again." Or, you can use time to practice forgiveness. With statements like, "It will be a joyous day on Earth the moment I choose to forgive you." One use imprisons you both; the other releases you both.

The ego is very tricky. It keeps you afraid but does not want you to question your fear because if you did, you would see that it stands on nothing solid. I believe that there is a common source of all dis-ease: We are afraid of who we are, because deep down we believe we are what our guilt tells us. In short, the ego uses time solely as a tool for making continual guilt until you believe it is who you are. See through this crazed thinking. You are not the person your guilt tells you that you are.

The part of your mind that wants peace is strong. It can undo all of the insanity of guilt right now. Think of the present as a doorway to a world that is clean of all your judgments. As you step through this doorway, light extends forever in all directions. Guilt is impossible here, while happiness is natural.

Time does not need to be your enemy anymore. Though it is true that it has taken time to accumulate your guilt, it takes only an instant to release by turning it over to God. This is how to experience love in the moment.

> *It is only possible to find the peace of the present moment when you become determined to hold nobody to the past with chains of guilt.*

INSTEAD OF SEEKING APPROVAL AND ACCEPTANCE, GIVE IT.

When fear fills you with self-doubt you can believe that the only solution is getting approval and acceptance. If they don't come, your feelings of low self-esteem increase. If they do, it is only a short time before you feel you must prove yourself again. This is the way of the ego.

This process begins early in life. I remember my junior high school dance: Boys were on one side, girls on the other, light dancing off the mirror ball hanging from the middle of the auditorium ceiling. Loud music was playing through buzzing speakers, the floors were sticky from spilled soft drinks held in nervous hands. My twelve year-old heart pounded in my chest at the mere thought of asking a girl to dance. Questions flooded my thoughts: "Do I look totally stupid in this shirt? Why, of all nights, do I have a zit the size of Mount Everest on the middle of my chin tonight? What will I do if she says 'yes'?"

Thirty years later, my ego can come up with the same questions, now worded for my adult mind: Is this book good enough? What will I look like if I keep losing my hair? Am I successful enough? The mirror ball is gone, wrinkles have replaced zits, but the fearful part of my mind still wants to go to the same places of self-doubt. Fortunately, I now have a way to stop all this nonsense.

Attitudinal Healing brings peace of mind through giving to others what you want for yourself. When you stop looking for what is wrong with yourself and other people and start looking for the spark of light in us all, your self-image improves. It is impossible to be judgmental of other people and not open yourself up to self-doubt, or feel an increased need to defend yourself. Similarly, it is impossible to extend love and acceptance to other people and not feel good about yourself. Simply put: *If you want to build your self-esteem, offer acceptance.*

In extending acceptance and approval don't focus on the persons "negative behavior." Instead, concentrate on the person's heart—what God created in perfect love. This theme runs through all of the principles of Attitudinal Healing.

Because some behavior can be very appalling, seeing the person's heart can be quite challenging. In various positions as a psychologist I have worked with people who have committed the worst of crimes. Certainly in those cases, my job wasn't to approve of their behavior. However, I do feel that a large part of my job was to see beyond their behavior and into their hearts. To essentially say, "You are accountable for your behavior, *and* I can see to the light beyond it." This was not always easy, but I always noticed that when I was successful I also felt loved. I believe this is because we have all done things or acted in ways that we are not proud of, and when we can see beyond another person's behavior we are also seeing beyond our own.

*When you recognize the light of
love in others you see it in yourself.*

The word "intimacy" is best understood as "in-to-me-see." There is a part of you that yearns to be fully known for who you are, and to fully know others. Listen to it.

You don't have to be a rocket scientist to understand one of the fundamentals of peace of mind: *When you are being controlling, intimacy is impossible.*

When you attempt to be controlling you are essentially saying, "I will only accept and love you if you behave as I want." It is a mistake to believe that this type of conditional love will make you happy.

My friend, Franklin Levinson, and myself have been teaching leadership and relationship skills to corporations, challenged youth, mental health organizations, and the general public using horses. Horses are great teachers about what happens to a relationship when control or domination is used. A horse will always give an honest response to what is presented to it, including yourself. You cannot hide from a horse, and in this they give you their greatest gift. With a horse, you must choose whether to control through force (from fear), or to join through trust, respect, knowledge, and mutual agreement (from love). One way produces a captive—a being whose actions are motivated by fear of disapproval or punishment. The other way produces a willing partner, a loyal and trusted equal. A friend.

A horse is always ready to be our willing and loyal partner, but only to the degree we are willing to do three things:

1. Be seen for who we are and be genuine with our emotions.

2. Be honest in the present moment.

3. Seek to understand and be patient.

Like horses, humans need to experience safety, respect, and patience in order to have trust and intimacy. In all my communications I try to remember:

> The desire to understand brings intimacy.
>
> Controlling prevents it.
>
> Giving from the heart creates trust.
>
> Controlling prevents it.

Being controlling can take many forms: manipulating with guilt, emotional and physical intimidation, playing the victim, rage and anger, money, sex, promises, threats, conditional love, being a martyr, complaining, not expressing feelings, among others.

Once you recognize that controlling others won't give you what you really want, you can begin to practice kindness, acceptance, and understanding.

*Communicate with patience and gentleness
and you will create safety and security.*

EVERY HOUR SEND
A LOVING THOUGHT.

Consider the action of sending loving thoughts as "happiness insurance." It's free, and even better, you receive dividends from what you give.

I believe that all the wisdom of the worlds spiritual teachings are held in four words: Extend love, receive love. There are a thousand ways to distract yourself from these four words, such as becoming too busy, holding onto the past, or harshly judging others. However, there is always one way to return: Choose to do so.

Imagine the world if every person, no matter what was going on, paused each hour and sent a loving thought. Let it begin with you today.

The means to be happy is with you every minute: Send a loving thought.

NOW IS THE ONLY TIME THERE IS, AND EACH INSTANT IS FOR GIVING.

6

We can learn to love ourselves and others by forgiving rather than judging.

When you judge others, you don't define them, you define yourself as someone who needs to judge and compartmentalize people.

. . . The highest spiritual act in life is to see yourself in everyone else and everyone else in you, to surrender yourself and see everyone's joy and suffering as your own, to detach yourself from your ego-need to be attached to the fruits of your labor, and to simply see everyone else in the world as part of you.

—Dr. Wayne Dyer

Some people's idea of forgiveness is, "bring the S.O.B. in so I can forgive him."

—Dr. William Thetford

DO YOU WANT TO BE ANGRY OR DO YOU WANT TO BE HAPPY?

Ironically, I just spent a good deal of time writing this section when my computer unexpectedly shut down, losing all of my work. After staring in disbelief at my darkened screen my first reaction was anger and blame. My anger was initially directed toward my antiquated computer for not working, and thus ruining my morning. My second reaction was to blame myself—for not saving the information, and for not coughing up the money for an updated computer long ago.

Does this sound like I was happy? Obviously not. But despite what part of my mind wanted me to believe, the real reason I was not happy had nothing to do with the unexpected event.

My unhappiness was due to the thoughts I was having, *not* the event that occurred. This was good news, because then I could do something about being unhappy.

When something goes "wrong" in life, your first reaction might be similar to mine: anger and blame. I, as you, can attest that neither of these will lead to being happy. They may lead to feeling right, dominating, or self-righteous, but don't confuse these feelings with happiness.

To be happy, it is important to learn to let go of blame

and anger as quickly as possible. This is not to say that you should expect to never experience anger, or that if you do, you have failed on your spiritual path. Rather, the intention is not to be taken by your anger and thus abandon your inherent happiness.

When my dog has a splintering, sharp bone in her mouth and I try to take it away, she chomps down harder. She does not recognize how dangerous it is for her. Humans and anger are much the same as dogs and bones. I have been amazed by how many people don't want to let go of anger, even when it is depriving them of living a full life. This is because the fearful part of our minds, our ego, tells us that our anger will keep us safe. The ego states that without anger, we will be taken advantage of, become unmotivated, and appear weak. If you look closely at this belief you will discover it is quite insane. *Holding onto anger actually keeps you unhappy, feeling alone, and unsafe.*

You may protest, "Well, I have every reason to be angry!" From one standpoint, who doesn't have reasons to be angry? It is certainly not difficult to look around this world and find plenty to be very angry about. Many arguments are even about who has the greater reason to be angry. What a waste of time! Would it not make more sense to spend your time arguing for your happiness?

Though you may not realize it, you are always choosing between two ways of perceiving: Looking to the world for reasons to be upset, or looking to your heart, to God, for reasons to be happy. I guarantee you will find what you are looking for.

To quote the Dalai Lama: *"The only factor that can give you refuge or protection from the destructive effects of anger and hatred is your practice of tolerance and patience."* Try to remember:

Patience and tolerance bring you happiness.

Anger and hatred bring you suffering.

If you find yourself stuck in anger, I suggest taking these three steps.

First, say to yourself, "I don't want this. There is another way." You may want to recognize the suffering your anger has caused you by closing your eyes and picturing yourself during times when you have been very angry. You may also want to recognize the suffering of those who have directly and indirectly received your anger. Don't do this to make yourself feel guilty. Do it to help make your decision to do something different.

Second, ask yourself, "Who am I angry with, and what are the ways they must have suffered in their lives?" Asking this sincerely will allow your heart to open to compassion and your mind to develop patience. You might also ask yourself, "What is my anger and lack of forgiveness costing me?"

Third, ask yourself, "What is human nature and what is God?" This step is larger, and can also be of benefit during times when you are not angry. I believe that as we do this, we begin to see that humans are inherently loving beings, having been created by a loving and forgiving God. Often, we become lost and forget who we are. Being lost we become fearful, and often find ourselves in endless cycles of attack and defense. The response that will bring us home is not anger and upset, but love and understanding.

It is interesting how if you are open and willing to release your anger, what first appeared to be wrong in your life can be transformed to a gift. Before my computer went off and I lost my information, I was trying to think of a story to illustrate the choice between anger and being happy. Now I have one.

Look to your heart and find reasons to be happy instead of looking to the past and to the world for reasons to be upset.

How could you not be afraid if you believed that every mistake you made was a reason to be guilty? When you don't realize your true nature is held safe for you, beyond all time and beyond all mistakes you have made, you become fearful.

The fearful part of your mind comes up with all sorts of crazy games it wants you to play. Your happiness is dependent on recognizing and ceasing to play these games. One of the most ludicrous games is based on the idea that making another person feel guilty, or suffer in any way, will make you feel better. I call this the game of Hot Potato. Below you will find the "rule book."

THE EGO'S GAME OF HOT POTATO

Overview of Game:

The goal of the game is to make another player, or a circumstance, responsible for your misery. In order to get rid of anything you don't want to look at within yourself, you quickly "throw" it to the closest available target, as you would if somebody tossed you something too hot to hold. It is permissible to blame anything you can think of, though double points are given when you find a single person or thing you can blame for everything.

Rules:

1. All players must pretend they can be something other than love. It is permissible for players to believe that at one time they were of pure heart, as long as they pretend their past behavior has replaced light with darkness.

2. Every player must try to pass all feelings of guilt or shame onto one of the other players or situations that appear on the board of life.

3. The player who can take the least responsi bility, and use blame and avoidance the most effectively, earns the most points.

4. When you are not tossing the hot potato of guilt, defend yourself against another person's. Advanced players will find it challenging to attempt to toss their guilt to another player while simultaneously defending themselves *and* planning future strategy.

5. If you do not toss the guilt, you must keep it your-self. Having these as your only choices motivates you to toss (i.e., blame) and keep the game going. It is *not* permissible to let go of the guilt and shame because if you were to do this you would see the power of forgiveness. Then there would be no motivation in continuing any of the ego's games.

Fear Cards:

After each turn the player must pick up a fear card. Players can try to get rid of their fear cards by either sneaking them into another player's hand, or attaching them to the guilt when tossing to the next player. Players can also try to hide their fear cards under the board and then pretend they have none.

Number of Players and Team Formation:

There is no limit to the number of players. You can form teams as long as the team members agree to have enemies. The game can become even more interesting if individual team members blame each other for any losses. Extra points are available for players who switch teams and then blame the former team for their problems. In teams of two this is often referred to as "divorce."

When you are participating in the game of Hot Potato, it can seem that there is no other alternative. Yet there is always a peaceful alternative. Hugh Prather, in his book *A Book of Games: A Course in Spiritual Play*, offers spiritual solutions to all of fear's games. One of my favorites is partially cited below. I have used it for years and find it is the perfect way out when I catch myself playing Hot Potato.

BALLS OF LIGHT: A LIGHT GAME[1]

Over your shoulder, the Master has placed a container that looks very much like a quiver or small golf bag. It contains balls of light each about the size of a snowball. There is an

[1]From A *Book of Games: A Course in Spiritual Play* by Hugh Prather, copyright © 1981 by Hugh Prather. Used by permission of Doubleday, a division of Random House, Inc.

ample supply and every ball of light is within easy reach. When you remove one, it will appear to others that you are only scratching your neck or brushing something from your shoulder.

Whenever you toss up and catch one of these balls, it automatically doubles in size. Consequently, it is possible to make as large a ball of light as you desire by simply juggling it awhile. Since the light is pure, even one small ball is enough, yet please make the light as large as you think is needed to do the job you have in mind, and use as many of them as you believe will be helpful.

You may toss a ball of light at anyone or anything you wish. If it is very large, you may send it with both hands as you would pass a basketball or bounce it off your forehead like a soccer ball. You can drop kick it or punt it. It is so light you can even blow it or flip it with your finger. So use any means of delivery you wish.

Once it arrives, it will surround and completely fill the person, animal, building, or whatever you have targeted and will cause it to shine and shine until all you can see will be lovely to look at, healed, and made so very happy.

Please observe this one rule: After you have finished, make for yourself an identically sized ball, toss it above your head, and let it settle over you, around you, and throughout you until you too glow as happily as the person or thing you have just blessed.

If you wish to use the balls of light for your own physical healing, the following procedure may prove helpful. First send the light to anyone, anywhere, whom you imagine having a similar difficulty. Then let the light represent your gift of forgiveness for anyone you may think deserves punishment, however slight. And after you recognize the gentle joy you feel on becoming completely harmless, let the ball of healing light touch and encompass your body and fill your heart and mind.

Choose the games you play carefully.
Your happiness depends on it.

THINK OF GOD AS A
GOOD DRY CLEANER.

A good dry cleaner is one you trust to remove just about any stain. You know you can bring the garment to your dry cleaner and it will be good as new. You have confidence even when you look at last Thanksgiving's dinner spilled down the front of your best outfit (the one that has been stuffed in the back of your closet for months). If you happen to have an occasional garment that for some reason doesn't come all the way clean, you don't quit taking your stained clothes to your dry cleaner and walk around filthy. You allow him to try again, or make some other suggestion.

God is in the stain removal business too. If you bring your painful emotions and past mistakes to Him, He removes them. Instead of same day service, He offers same moment service. His magic is in that he doesn't even see the stain you think is so big, so it disappears.

It cannot be emphasized enough that if you are walking around with anything other than peace of mind, it is because you have not chosen to bring your unforgiving thoughts to God.

Your negative emotions are like well-baited hooks waiting for you to bite. There are two stages of upset where it is most helpful to ask for God's help.

First, ask for assistance to not take the bait. When you are tempted to judge, ask Him to offer you a different perception. When you are tempted to be angry, ask Him to give you understanding and compassion. When you are suffering in any way, ask for His gentle words to guide you. Asking for this kind of help is like seeing a storm coming and deciding to seek refuge instead of running directly into it.

Second, when you have already taken the well-baited hook, perhaps having said or done something you wish you had not, ask God for the strength to stop and listen to what else you might think and how else you might behave. Don't dig a deeper hole for yourself by continuing down the same road when it isn't bringing you what you want. Remember, progress on a spiritual path is nothing more than being able to turn to God where previously you would have only listened to your fear and escalated in your upset.

> *God the dry cleaner: Same moment*
> *service, always open, never a cost. Now,*
> *there's a deal for the new millennium.*

Around my house, I can get busy and forget (or procrastinate) to take out the trash. Yesterday morning, I found myself with my foot in the kitchen trash can, trying to stuff just one more old milk carton in, rather than making the trip out to the garbage can. I stepped on one of my kid's old half-empty juice boxes, squirting warm, sticky liquid up the leg of my pants. I had to change clothes, wash my leg, and launder the pants. The two-minute walk to take out the garbage would have been much easier.

Similarly, this stuffing process can happen mentally. I can let negative or old thoughts directed at myself and others pile up, and not take the time to let go of them. If I keep stuffing without letting go, something sticky and smelly (like anger) usually squirts out. Then I have a mess to clean up. The few minutes a day it takes to practice forgiveness makes for a much easier life.

I have found that forgiveness practice sessions greatly help to keep my mind clear of thoughts that don't bring me peace. I suggest that once a day, beginning today, you schedule five-minute forgiveness sessions. During this time your task is to think about the people in your life, including yourself, and to see beyond their behavior and into who they are. Imagine their (or your) behavior is like whitecaps on the surface of the ocean. Look beyond the weather and the waves, and into the depths of the water. Visualize a glimmer of light in their hearts, a gentle smile (which even they may be unaware of). Do the same with yourself. Each session let this light grow brighter, and the smile wider. Undertaking this practice will make you remarkably lighter and happier. People around you will notice the difference too.

The following will help clarify what to focus on during your practice sessions, as well as the importance of doing them.

> Forgiveness does *not* mean that you condone all behaviors, or stop holding others accountable for their actions.

> Forgiveness does mean that you are willing to look for the light of God in everybody.

> Forgiveness is a result of seeing yourself and other people in the present moment, absent of the past.

> Forgiveness is choosing to see the light of God in somebody whom you are tempted to judge.

> Forgiveness is the foundation for your happiness. Practicing it will change your life completely.

Forgiveness can be misunderstood. The fearful part of your mind can come up with many reasons not to forgive.

Choose not to listen to the unforgiving voice and instead remember:

When you forgive you see the love that is within people, no matter how well hidden by their unbecoming behavior.

When at the movies you may become very involved in the film, even to the point of having physical and emotional reactions, such as crying or a pounding heart. Yet, all the while, there is a part of your mind that knows you are at the movies, watching a drama unfold in front of you. You never lose the ability to turn your head away, or leave altogether.

There are movies going on all the time in the theater of your mind. The film is your thoughts. In this theater, you often behave as if the movie is real and that there is nothing you can do about your experience. You sit and experience angry, revengeful, and frightening movies and don't realize that you are the writer, director, and projectionist.

Attitudinal Healing helps you to recognize that you have the ability to change the film! To do this, you need to learn how to be aware of your thoughts without allowing them to run wild. Developing the ability to watch and identify your thoughts gives you tremendous freedom.

The process of thought-watching is akin to going through the movie listings and deciding what film you want to see. Certainly, it would be a sad state of affairs if you wanted to see a love story or comedy, but believed that all you were permitted to see were horror films.

Many meditation techniques stress the importance of being able to develop the ability to watch your thoughts without attachment to them. Many psychologists have also found that this is an excellent skill to develop, because people are then more easily able to see the root causes of their suffering, *and* be able to do something about it.

Some forms of Buddhism call this practice "Bystander Mind." The idea is that there is a part of your mind which can watch the rest of your mind. You watch your thoughts as you would watch waves at the beach, coming in, going out. There might be some calm times without many waves, and you just watch the calm. There might be other times with large, crashing waves, and you just watch the dramatic display. But in all observing you don't become attached.

When watching your thoughts remember:

> You are at the movies. Don't act like all of your horror films and action thrillers are real. Remember, only love is real.

> Know that you can change films any time. You can even rewrite the scripts. Themes of fear and revenge can be switched to themes of love and forgiveness at any time you choose.

> Begin to spend time looking at the movie listings prior to going to the movies. Choose your thoughts. The best times to

do this are before you get out of bed, and
before you go to sleep.

The following is a simple technique to get you started on developing a bystander mind. Practicing this daily will lead you to be the ruler of your own mind.

Sit with your eyes closed and watch your thoughts as though they were leaves on a stream floating past you. Don't reach into the water and grab any one of them. Instead, name them as they float by. Try to have a mental stance that is as detached as possible. Simply watch your thoughts and state what it is about. Suppose, for example, that you are thinking about a money problem. Say to yourself, "Thinking about money," and then move on to whatever else comes into your mind. Try to resist the temptation of delving into any one thought. If you do, simply catch yourself, name the thought, and move onto the next.

Don't be discouraged if this technique takes some time to develop. Taming an unruly mind takes patience and perseverance. The payoff is you get to choose the movies.

Become the director of your own mind.
Peace is a choice that only you can make.

SEE BEYOND IMPERFECTION.

Some kimonos (Japanese robes) have a design and purpose that is very different from western clothes. Certain robes are very plain on the outside, and even have imper fections purposely sewn into them. On the inside they are intricately beautiful and meticulously crafted. I imagine the purpose of the robe is to remind the wearer that their beauty lies within. Those who see the robe being worn, with only the imperfect outside visible, are reminded to think of the magnificence beneath the exterior—of the robe, the person, and themselves.

If all you see is imperfection—I'm too fat, they're unfair, you're not attractive enough—it is the same as focusing only on the outside of the kimono. There is always the option to shift your focus and see the loveliness of what is in the heart.

Looking to what is on the inside of the kimono, beyond the imperfection, is precisely what forgiveness is. When you are able to look beyond the mistakes and imperfections of people and recognize their magnificence, you have prac ticed forgiveness.

In reference to forgiveness, I often hear the comment, "My (parent, spouse, etc.) has never really expressed their love for me. We barely talk anymore. Do you think that there is a chance that if I offer them blessings and forgiveness they will change?" This question points to the belief that, for forgiveness to be worthwhile, the other person needs to change in some way. Instead, look within yourself. Forgiveness is your most powerful tool for healing because with forgiveness you always receive blessings—even if the person's behavior does not change. This is because:

When you behold another with the eyes of love, you see your own magnificence too.

We are a culture obsessed with youth. Billions of dollars are spent every year on wrinkle creams, facelifts, tummy tucks, breast implants, and the like.

I may not have a choice about getting wrinkles, but I do have a choice in how they are developed. When I am ninety, I want to have deep lines around my eyes from countless moments of joy. I want those smiles to have come from knowing how much I am loved by God and how much love I have to give. I want to have upturned lines around my mouth from holding a gentle smile for all humanity for at least a few hours each day. I want my hands to be creased from years of touching and giving to others. I want my forehead to be lined with thoughtfulness and free from frowns. I want my arms to have worked hard in both reaching out and in receiving. I want my heart to be alive with love the moment it ceases to beat, and trust that love will live forever.

I am not sure how marketable it would be in a climate where people pay big bucks to get rid of their wrinkles, but what about a Smile-Wrinkle Development Program? Instead of creams and surgeries, the focus would be on thoughts and attitudes. Every morning and evening, and as much time during the day as possible, you would think thoughts that make you smile. Below are a few examples. Begin your Smile-Wrinkle Development Program today by practicing these thoughts and making some up for yourself.

- To everyone I offer joy, gentleness, and peace.

- I will receive what I am giving now.

- The peace of God radiates in and around me.

- Forgiveness is my only goal today.

- Being happy is natural and important.

Positive expressions and feelings are contagious—you see someone smile and it tends to make you feel good and smile yourself. Start an epidemic of smile-wrinkles in your family and community.

The only real elixir for becoming ageless is loving-kindness. It can't be bought, but it can be given and received.

7

We can become love finders rather than fault finders.

It is essential to continue to go in the direction of peace and love, even when we don't succeed in that goal, every moment of every day.

—Gerald Jampolsky, M.D.,
in *Love is the Answer*

Man invented language for his deep need to complain.

—Lily Tomlin

HOLD A GRUDGE,
HOLD YOURSELF BACK.

When you hold a grudge, you have the idea that punishing the other person will somehow make you feel better. You may even wish for their suffering. Let's examine this insane thinking.

In reality, holding a grudge makes you unavailable to new positive experiences because you are holding onto old negative ones. The really crazy part about this is that, assumably, you are holding a grudge because you didn't like what happened, and yet you keep the negative experience alive in the present by holding the grudge. *Having grudges is like laying out footsteps to follow to repeated unhappiness.* This, ultimately, is punishing *yourself*.

Think of your mind as a container that you can fill with grudges and judgments, or with love and forgiveness. Every grudge leaves a little less room for the awareness of love. Step back from what you are angry or hurt about and ask, "What do I want to fill my mind with?"

If you had a case of "celestial amnesia," where you had forgotten any grudges and unforgiving thoughts you may have once had, how would you feel? When you cease to hold grudges, something is freed up inside of yourself. To stop holding yourself back—give up grudges.

In truth, we have each been given the gifts of God. He

has held nothing back that can bring you happiness. If you are busy carrying grudges you won't have room to receive these gifts. For myself, when I have been holding grudges, God's gifts went unnoticed because I valued my anger more.

When you value anger, the world is upside down: God's gifts appear dangerous and grudges look like they will create safety. The good news is that God's gifts never disappear while you wander in this insanity. When you are willing to give up valuing grudges, you discover love waiting patiently for you. Whenever the ego preaches about all you have to be angry with, God is whispering, "Let it go." Where holding a grudge chains you to unhappiness, giving the gift of forgiveness sets you free.

If you choose to focus on grudges, you won't have much time to create positive outcomes for your life. Ask a pessimist if he has any grudges, and the list of them will be long. Ask an optimist, and the list is probably nonexistent. Which do you want to be?

It is impossible to hold a grudge and have peace of mind at the same time. It would be like trying to have day and night exist in the same moment.

While writing this book someone asked me, "If you could only have one of the vignette titles to live by, which would it be?" Though I think they are all important, what the philosopher Aldous Huxley said at the end of his life moves me. Following a lifetime in pursuit of truth, when asked what was most important, he is reported to have said, "After all the years of studying philosophy it is a bit embarrassing that upon departing this world I have little other advice than, 'Be a little kinder than you need to be.'"

You could put this book down now, never read another word of philosophy, religion, or psychology, and do wonderfully well spiritually by living the truth contained in Huxley's one sentence.

At the most basic level, the large problems of the world have one simple solution. What is the answer to prejudice? Kindness. To environmental problems? Kindness. To problems or misunderstanding in your family? Kindness.

Imagine your life if you were a little kinder at home, with people at work, and with strangers. I am not talking about acts that require any sacrifice at all: Perhaps smile at the clerk who seems to be having a bad day. Spend a few minutes of listening to your children, with an attitude that they are the most incredible beings you have ever experienced. Give a few dollars or a few hours to a charity.

Kindness comes naturally when you direct your thoughts to recognize how important it is. Your mind can be like fertile land that has been ignored. Before you can expect anything beautiful to grow, you need to cultivate it lovingly. The following are some "cultivating thoughts" that will lead your mind and actions toward kindness:

> The heart of everyone you meet is deserving of kindness.

> Holding on to anger and resentments will not bring you what you want.

> Withholding kindness is a decision to suffer.

> It is to your benefit to be kind.

> Nothing good comes from punishing yourself.

> Kindness leads to happiness. You deserve to be happy.

> The hardest time to be kind is when you feel attacked. It is also the most important. See people who are attacking as fearful, and in need of love.

> It is easier to be kind when you focus on a person's heart rather than their behavior.

Everyone, including you, has an innocent child living in them who deserves your kindness.

It is easier to be kind when you focus on your blessings, rather than your hurts.

Judgments are roadblocks to kindness.

Patience is the doorway to kindness.

Your thoughts are like a boomerang. Your judgments and unforgiving thoughts will most certainly return and whack you in the back of the head. Instead:

Make the decision to extend kindness and feel the warmth of love replace everything else.

GIVE YOURSELF THE
GIFT OF QUIET TIME.

When a pond is stirred up, the water becomes murky. If allowed to sit still, clarity will gradually return as the sediment settles. The same is true with your mind. Without giving yourself times of stillness and quiet on a regular basis, your mind will not be clear and your decisions and perceptions will be clouded.

A corporate executive I was working with was telling me how she was able to do many things at once, and how this skill is what had saved her many times. I commented to her that, though this is a useful trait some of the time, if you are always in this mode, there is something wrong with the picture. I suggested to her that being able to do nothing and be still is equally, if not more, important.

People who are too busy, over-stressed, and take no time for stillness tend to become fault finders. They always see what is wrong. People who take time for quiet reflection tend to be more able to see through loving eyes.

If you buy into the overemphasis on materialism and achievement in our culture, you will be led to a life of spiritual deprivation. A balance between accomplishment and awareness of the more subtle parts of life—your own heartbeat, the sound of the wind, children playing—is the indicator of a healthy life.

Most people don't have this important balance as they grow up. The majority of schools are task-oriented, and few teach how to have a still mind. Few families emphasize stillness with their busy schedules. I grew up in a family where our appearance to the world was very important. Much of the time, there was more emphasis on what I was doing than on who I was. In other words, *doing* was more important than *being*. It was not until a few years after receiving my doctorate in my early twenties that I began to see that I had become very good at accomplishing tasks, but did not know much about being still. During the last twenty-five years, I have continued to see the value of quiet time each day. However, quiet time does not always come easy. There have been many times when I have created the space for still reflection, only to fill up that space with tasks that seem all too important at the time. I have come to see that, each year, I do a little better at maintaining uninterrupted space, and for this I am grateful. And when my tricky mind sneaks its "to do" list into my quiet space, I try and have a sense of humor about it, as though I am training a puppy who has a very short attention span.

There are two types of quiet time that are important. One was described above, and can be built into your day: Perhaps fifteen minutes in the morning and evening for meditation, contemplation, and prayer. The other, described below, is learning to pause when you are upset.

When you are having a bad day, you probably don't realize that you have made a choice. Even though your reactions may feel automatic, there is always a thought behind them. In order to recognize these thoughts and be able to do something different, be willing to pause and reflect. Most of the time when people are having a bad day, they do things and think thoughts that are the equivalent of throwing fuel on flames. Instead, learn to use any upset as a cue for you to pause. Tell yourself, "There is another way to see this. I am *not* a robot, and I don't have to react in any particular way."

Don't fool yourself into thinking that when you are upset you should always do something. If you are honest with yourself, probably your worst decisions and actions have come from being upset. The best course of action when you are upset is to take time to pause and be still, *before you respond.*

When it comes to taking quiet time most people have the tendency to procrastinate, seeing other tasks as more important. Don't. Your peace of mind depends on it.

> *Having time each day for being*
> *still is a prerequisite for peace*
> *of mind and clarity of vision.*

Most of us like to think that our perception and memory are accurate, airtight, and without a flaw. We rarely question what our eyes and mind show us. Yet the hard truth is that our memory is about as reliable as a weather forecast for next month.

Even when something is happening right in front of us our thoughts will often lead to a perception that is false. The most basic facts of a situation are often not reported as they actually occurred, let alone the emotional content, motivation, or reasoning behind them. I recall a study where a robbery was staged in front of a group of fifteen people. The "robber" quickly entered the room, yelled a few words, made a few demands, and then left. Next, each witness was asked individually what had happened, as well as basic information such as height, clothing, and hair color. As you might have guessed, there were fifteen different descriptions. Based on the eyewitnesses, the robber had either blond or brown hair, was between five-nine and six-three, was between thirty-two and forty-five, and was wearing either jeans or blue slacks. Not even his race could be agreed upon. When more subjective questions were posed, such as what might have motivated the robber, the responses were even more diverse.

Despite the unreliability of our perception and memory, we can rely heavily upon false perceptions to pass judgment. Marriages end, parents and children stop speaking, friendships are broken, all based on something very undependable.

There is an alternative way to process information that isn't "memory dependent": Ask God to show you what He would have you see and how He would have you respond.

At first, it can be unsettling to think that what you believe happened probably didn't. Yet, if your goal is to be a love finder and not a fault finder, then the details don't really matter. In fact, being able to see beyond the details is central. What is important is really wanting to respond compassionately to all situations. When this is your goal, you look for reasons to love rather than to find fault. For example, in the robbery illustration you would ask yourself, "What suffering could this person have gone through in their life that would lead them to this act?"

The phrase, "What you believe will happen probably will," is an acknowledgment that your thoughts are powerful and are always creating. There is, of course, no guarantee that visualizing that promotion you want will bring it to fruition, or that seeing a person recovering from a chronic illness will always lead to it come true, but there is no doubt that such visualization increases the odds. Cancer research has demonstrated that those who have an optimistic outlook for their illness do far better than those who see themselves suffering and then dying.

More importantly, when it comes to your own *reactions* and *feelings,* visualizing can work miracles. If you were to spend even a few minutes every day picturing yourself having peace of mind, even in difficult situations, you would find yourself much more consistently happy. In contrast, if you spend time excessively worrying and thinking of how angry you will be of this or that happens, you will likely find yourself in a life with very little happiness.

You are perceiving a situation wrongly if you are experiencing something other than compassion.

LOOK FOR SIMILARITIES
RATHER THAN DIFFERENCES.

The ego loves to occupy itself with finding differences. There appears to be a need in the world to reduce everything to right or wrong, rather than opening to the similarities people share.

When I was in graduate school I discovered that most research focused on the differences between theories, philosophies, and ideas. Few people seemed very interested in universal truths.

This way of thinking is reflective of our culture's tendency to divide in order to understand. Though such an approach can be useful at certain stages of inquiry, without balance, it leads to greater separation between people, religions, and fields of study. The environment suffers because when differences are focused upon, the interconnectedness of life can be overlooked. This leads to the dangerous belief that altering one part will have no effect on the whole. Certainly, environmental destruction has tragically taught the falsity of this thinking.

In my life, I try to focus less on differences and more on similarities. I like to ask questions such as: "Is there a common thread that runs through all spiritual traditions? What do all hearts share?" These questions lead me to see the world as incredibly interconnected, where love is the universal language.

Seeing differences or similarities reflects two very different ways of approaching the world. One is through fear and the other is through love.

The fearful part of your mind focuses on differences, primarily using the past as its source of information. Fear tells you that unconditional love is dangerous. By dividing the world into little parts—skin color, religion, ethnicity, education, socio-economic status, political orientation—the ego tells you that you will come to understand more and be safe. But the real purpose of all separation is to "seek but do not find." *The ego's tool of separation will never lead to peace of mind.*

Fear-based approaches to the world always look for differences through separation. The five core principles the ego uses in life are:

1. Control your surroundings and be safe.

2. Analyze all situations.

3. Use the past to judge.

4. Dominate the environment.

5. If you feel threatened, attack.

In contrast, love focuses on similarities and primarily uses the present as its source of information. When you choose love as your guide and look for how hearts are the same, a whole different world opens up. Fear vanishes because there is no reason for it to exist. Through loving, you ultimately recognize that all minds are joined in God.

The five core principles love uses in life are:

1. Love and be safe.

2. Listen gently.

3. Accept others in the moment.

4. Respect all life.

5. Forgive.

Think about the different experiences that come from the principles of fear and love. I suggest you write down the five principles of fear on one side of a card, and the five of love on the other. Carry it with you. Several times a day, especially if you feel upset in any way, read both sides of the card and choose which you want to follow. It is impossible to do both at the same time. This exercise will help you tremendously in seeing what it is you choose between, and will help you exchange fault finding for love finding.

Love-based approaches to the world always look for similarities through compassion rather than separating though fear.

DO EVERYTHING A LITTLE MORE GENTLY THAN USUAL.

Being gentle is a reflection of a peaceful mind and loving heart. Like all compassionate acts, this works in reverse, too—being gentle will bring you a loving heart and a peaceful mind. If you want happiness, it makes sense to increase your ability to be gentle.

The first step in becoming gentler is seeing no value in harm. You cannot be harmful and be gentle. Harmfulness will make you feel confused, guilty, and angry. Ultimately it will make you untrusting, defensive, and suspicious.

If you see that absolutely no gain can come from being harmful in any way, then you have all the room in the world to be gentle. In fact, gentleness comes naturally to the mind that sees no reason to harm anyone or anything.

Sometimes in daily living it is easy to become like a bull in a china shop. The need for gentleness can be overlooked despite the fact that things are breaking around you. Perhaps your relationship crashes and breaks, or people become leery or afraid of you in some way. Or, perhaps you have been doing the same job, or have been in the same relationship for so long that you have simply forgotten the need to be present and gentle.

I have seen some people who feel stuck in a rut with no way out change only one thing: They decide to be more present and gentle. They report that they immediately have more purpose and meaning in their life, and they have changed nothing except wanting to be gentler! So, before you make big changes in your life, first try just being gentler. You will be amazed at the results!

Some people mistakenly see gentleness as weakness. Though it is true that gentleness does not use force, it has its own strength. Christ, Buddha, Mother Teresa, and others were strong through being gentle. This strength is available to every one of us at all times. A great way to cultivate being a love finder is by practicing being gentle.

Being gentle is a natural outcome of being sensitive. With all the input from the world in today's culture it is easy to become guarded as a means of survival. You can put on your blinders in the morning before leaving the house, and see and feel very little during your day. Slowly, you can become cut off from the beauty in life because you desensitize yourself to the barrage of input of modern society. The following are examples of ways to increase your sensitivity, and thus become gentler:

- Walk in something soft with bare feet.

- Touch a face with your eyes closed.

- Watch the wind.

- Feel your breath in your nostrils as you inhale and exhale.

- Eat slowly and taste your food.

- Feel your heart while you smile.

- Smell flowers.

- Listen to water.

- Watch the moon rise.

- Touch a baby.

In addition to sensitivity exercises, spend an hour here and there (maybe even a day) being more gentle than usual as you go about your daily activities. Drive more fluidly. Speak as though your words would be the last words that person ever heard. Whatever your job is, bring gentleness to it. Find the light of people you are with in their eyes.

It is impossible to be gentle with yourself or other people when you are looking for fault or seeing any value in guilt.

When I was a kid I loved to camp. Still do. My favorite part is going to sleep at night, looking up at the stars. I can remember doing so at about sixteen years old, on top of a hill covered in golden grass on a warm summer night. It was then I had my first glimpse of the infinite. "How far does it go?" I asked myself as I gazed into the heavens. With this single question, my world would never be quite the same. I felt the anxiety and the wonder of what is infinite. I felt anxiety because there is a part of myself that wants to contain everything, make it small so that I can understand it. I felt wonder because there is a larger part of myself that knew for the first time that I was a part of the infinite that stretched out above me. I wasn't a kid on a hill looking into something, I was part of it. My problems suddenly didn't seem so big.

Much later in life, I began to have the same experience in meditation. I looked within myself, as though I were back on the hill gazing at the universe. "How far does my soul go?" I asked. Again I experienced the infinite and the magnitude of God. Then I asked, "How far does love reach? Is there a limit to the depths that I can love?" And again, the infinite brushed my mind.

In my daily life, I am not always experiencing the infinite, and sometimes I drop into making things very small and I become a fault finder. However, my experiences of the infinite help me to put things in perspective much more quickly than I once did. I find it helpful to take the time to continue touching the infinite so I am less likely to lock myself up in a small and confined world.

My words and my experiences cannot fully convey the infinite to you. So, I encourage you to spend time lying on your back and looking up at the stars. Also, sit quietly and look within. Maybe immediately, maybe with time, you will have the perspective that comes from experiencing the expanse of infinite love.

When you experience even a glimpse of the magnitude of love, all that you found fault with in the past will seem smaller than a grain of sand on a ten-mile beach.

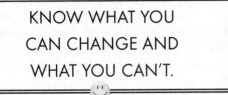

KNOW WHAT YOU CAN CHANGE AND WHAT YOU CAN'T.

Remember as a kid when you were asked, "If a genie gave you only one wish, what would it be?" You probably were not very old before you learned to quickly answer, "A million more wishes!"

Here is a similar question: "If you could change just one thing, what would it be?"

The answer that is equivalent to "a million more wishes" is, "My thoughts!" When you learn to look to your thoughts whenever you are upset in anyway, you have discovered true freedom, even beyond the genie's million wishes. You can always choose to redirect you thoughts.

Though the world isn't responsible for how you feel, you do have a part in creating outcomes. Most fault finding is done *after* something happens that you don't like. This is like going to a restaurant, demanding food without reading the menu, and then complaining about the food that is brought to you. Instead of saying, "Wow, I guess I should have thought about what I wanted," you blame the wait-person, the cook, and the establishment rather than seeing your part in the fiasco.

Have you ever been asked what you want in a situation,

and replied, "I'm not sure what I want to happen, but I sure know what I don't want." This is your ego speaking and showing its true colors. It only focuses on the negative, and has no idea about any positive outcome. The time to think about what you want to happen is at the beginning. Don't wait until the waitperson brings you the food and then complain. Ask yourself at the beginning of any situation that you are uncertain about, "What do I want to have happen?" Even more importantly, ask yourself, "What is the purpose of this situation?"

I worked with a man who was in a sales position. He was making excellent money, but was extremely stressed out. Every time he didn't make a sale he felt the weight of the world on his shoulders. I asked him to ponder this question, *prior to* each sales call: "What is the *real* purpose of this interaction?" To his surprise, his answers had nothing to do with making a sale! His answers kept being things like, "Be genuinely interested in this person." "Be patient and kind." "See their heart." His smile during his meetings changed from a fake one, worn by an over-stressed salesman, to a genuine one of a fellow human being. Not only did his stress disappear, his sales went up! Of course they did. Who would you rather be in a relationship with, business or personal, somebody who only wanted something from you, or somebody who clearly cared about you?

When you put a positive goal at the beginning of any situation it will determine the outcome. The ego does the opposite by going into a situation with no positive goal. It proceeds to find fault in whatever is going on, and then blames other people or circumstances when the outcome is something it deems less than satisfactory. Don't spend your life in this cycle of insanity! Stop looking back at what happened, feeling short-changed, or trying to figure out what went wrong. Instead, put your undivided attention on placing positive goals at the beginning—goals that are not based on the external but that have to do with your perception and personal actions. When you do this, you will acquire the ability to focus on the positive aspects (love finding) of a situation by overlooking any obstacles (fault finding) that get in your way.

Fault finding comes from believing
your happiness comes from the world
going according to your liking.

8

We can choose and direct ourselves to be peaceful inside regardless of what is happening outside.

Faced with a crisis that demands resolution . . . you need to search for the potential for spiritual growth inherent in the situation.

Caroline Myss, Ph.D.,
in *Why People Don't Heal*

This saying reminds me that whenever I am thinking that something or somebody else is responsible for my happiness, I had best take a look at myself.

Finger-pointing doesn't go far in building anything positive because it lacks responsibility. Regardless what end of the pointed finger you are looking at, it doesn't feel good.

Over the years, I have been blessed to have some friends in my life who have demonstrated the power of asking, "What can *I* do that is positive?" instead of "Who is to blame for this?" They asked this during difficult times, not just when it was convenient to do so. As you read about them, remember that all they had was the willingness to ask the question, "What can I do?"—And then listen to the answer.

Patricia Qualls: In the early 1990's, when news broke about the problems of orphanages in Romania, most of us found plenty of people and countries to point our fingers at. The images of mistreated children made us wonder who was responsible. After a brief period of being angry and pointing her finger like the rest of us, Patty looked at the three fingers pointing back at her and asked, "What can I do?" Despite potential financial loss and the interruption of her career, she left for a year in Romania and became a major organizer and fundraiser, touching the lives of thousands of children.

Michael Rosenthal: Michael's lovely wife, Rosewitta, became ill and died in the prime of her life. Michael and his son, Toby, suffered great loss, as have many with an unexpected death. Michael could have become lost in blaming doctors for some mistakes, or God for his loss, but instead he looked at the three fingers pointing back to him and asked, "What can I do?" Today Michael has touched many with his heartfelt presence and his extended hand, helping finance The Center for Attitudinal Healing, serving hundreds of families going through the loss that he and Toby experienced.

Sharlene Hemmingway: Sharlene is like most people—she has to work and doesn't have much extra time. When she saw increasing numbers of homeless people on the streets, she could have blamed the economy, the government, or the individuals. She could have pointed at who should fix the problem. She could have looked past the homeless, not seeing their pain. Instead, she looked at the three fingers pointing at her and asked, "What can I do?" Over the last many years, she has organized donations and labor to feed and clothe thousands of homeless people.

Despite the time and effort it took for my friends to do what they did, they describe receiving so much more than they gave. We do not have to do something as large as my friends did, but their example serves as an inspiration to the miracles that can come when you ask, "What can I do?" rather than asking, "Who's fault is it?" Just think of the differences in your own family or relationship which this shift can make! When you hear the answer to the question, "What can I do?" you smile because you know you are directing your mind to the solution instead of being part of the problem.

Look to your own thoughts and actions,
instead of pointing your finger, and you
will feel less controlled by the world and
more able to direct your own life.

DEVELOP AN ATTITUDE
OF GRATITUDE.

It seems fitting that I am writing this vignette the day after Thanksgiving. Upon reflecting on all that I am thankful for, I find myself most grateful for the capacity to give and receive love. It is my guarantee that a positive outcome to all situations is possible.

In the past, I have spent so much time and energy examining what was missing in my life, what was wrong, and what could be improved upon that I overlooked the power of loving in the moment. A daily *attitude of gratitude* helps me to see clearly.

Being thankful makes good things happen. Gratitude is like a magical fertilizer that allows positive experiences to grow abundantly in your life. This Thanksgiving, I see more precisely than ever that *being happy has nothing to do with how much you have, and everything to do with how grateful you are for what you do have.*

There are two beliefs that lead to having deep gratitude:

1. Who you are is love. Love never abandons you, but you can choose to cover it with shame and guilt. When you cover up love, you pretend that it has vanished and that darkness is who you are.

But, as any child learns early on, you need only lift the cover to see what is underneath.

2. Every person wants to experience compassion and union. This recognition brings understanding and happiness to relationships. When you respond to this need in every person, even when you don't like their behavior, you create positive experiences.

When you believe in these two principles you are able to make every situation a lesson in learning to love more fully. You become grateful for all situations.

When I suggest you can be grateful for all situations because they can teach you about loving, I am not suggesting that you want "bad" things to happen. There is a difference between wanting something to happen and the ability to be grateful for it. For example, I didn't want to be severely hearing-impaired, but I am grateful for it because the disability has taught me so much about listening with the heart. I didn't want a divorce, but it taught me about loving deeply and about forgiveness, and for this I am grateful. I didn't want to be an addict at an early age, but I am grateful for my recovery because it taught me so much about where happiness comes from.

Resist the temptation to compare yourself with other people to figure out if you should be grateful or not. Comparison can be the destroyer of gratitude. Hatred, envy, and jealousy come from comparison and make gratitude very difficult.

Gratitude and love are linked together. Focus on either and you will have the other.

(*Gratitude is the "attitudinal password" that takes you through the doorway of your heart.*)

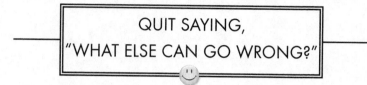

Have you ever noticed a tendency that, when your day doesn't go as well as planned, you might say, "What else can go wrong?" Yet, in response to positive occurrences you tend to say, "Boy, that'll never happen again." This is because your ego expects negative circumstances to follow negative circumstances, but believes you're just lucky if something positive happens.

To get an idea of how your thoughts create positive or negative responses, imagine yourself at the top of a snow-covered hill and you have just made a snowball about three feet in diameter. You give your ball a push, and down the hill it travels, picking up speed and size on its own. None of this would surprise you, of course, for you understand the nature of gravity. You also know that snowballs tend to get larger when they are rolled because snow sticks to itself.

Your mind works in a very similar manner. When you have a thought, and you give it a little energy, it will pick up momentum. Like the snowball, once your thought is on a roll it will take up more of your consciousness by attracting like-minded thinking. Negative thoughts stick to other negative thoughts. Let's say, for example, you are having an okay day. Suddenly your boss walks in, appearing to be having a bad day. She begins to point out whatever she thinks you are doing wrong, and then gives you a "priority project." After your boss leaves, you realize that you forgot your lunch and, with the extra work, you don't have time to go out today. You mutter under your breath, "What else can possibly go wrong?" Next, though you might not realize it, you begin looking for what is going to further mess up your day. Your mood goes sour, and maybe you even become a little like your boss was earlier, having a negative attitude with other people. This, in turn, gives you unwanted responses from your co-workers, which gives you all the more reason to continue your "bad day."

Your "bad day" didn't get started because of your surly boss or because you missed lunch. It happened because you had a thought that you gave a little shove at the top of a hill, and down it went, getting bigger with like-minded negative thoughts.

The good news is that once you begin to see this, there are a couple of ways to stop it. First, imagine you are back at the top of the snow-covered hill. This time, you notice there are two piles of snow to make your snowballs from. One is slightly dark, with a dingy appearance. The other is glistening white and sparkling in the sun. Over the dingy pile is the phrase, "Past pain and fear." Over the shimmering pile is the phrase, "Present joy and love." Imagine that the hill is your mind. Which snowballs do you want to send down it, growing along the way?

Second, if you overlooked your choice at the top of the hill and find that your negative thinking is already on a pretty good roll, imagine that you can get out in front of your dingy snowball-thinking and yell, "*Stop!*" It does. Of course it stops! The original thought was your creation. You gave it the energy to get it going. When you withdraw your energy from it, it ceases to exist.

What this is saying is that:

- You have control over your response to circumstances.

- When you look for what is wrong, you will find it.

- When you look for what is positive, you will find it.

- What you put energy into creates momentum.

- You can stop your negative thinking by choosing to do so.

- You should choose your piles of snow carefully.

Train your mind to be on the lookout for the positive. When good things happen say, "What else is going to go right today?"

The happiest lives are built on forgiveness, where we recognize ourselves as spiritual beings.

Consider that your only purpose is to give and receive loving-kindness. If you are not doing this, and are unhappy, you have likely taken on a role that does not serve you or other people.

You may not realize it, but you have a choice in what roles you take in life. When you feel stuck, or are repeating a pattern you wish you were not, you have chosen a role that you may want to reconsider. You don't have to accept every script that comes your way, and you can get rid of the roles that you no longer see any point in playing. The following is a partial list of common roles that you may want to decline or resign from.

- The tragic victim who tries, but is repeatedly hurt.

- The son or daughter who is never good enough.

- The person who is always trying to please so he will be loved.

- The person who starts, but never finishes.

- The rich person who is superior.

- The poor person who is inferior.

- The person who is always perfect.

- The stoic person who never feels emotion.

Notice what all of these roles have in common:

- They focus on the past and the future.

- They believe that happiness comes from the external.

- They believe that happiness is dependent on a good performance.

- The emphasis is on *what they do,* not *who they are.*

- They deny that they are spiritual beings.

The release from these roles comes from asking yourself, "How do I want to be right now?" Assuming that you don't want any roles similar to the above, you may want to answer, "I want to forgive myself and others." Take a look at the following example.

You are at your relatives' house for the holidays and a family member begins to say something that typically leads to you feeling upset. Instead of taking the role offered, as you have done countless times before, choose to see beyond their words. See only that they want to be loved. This is forgiveness, the gentle recognition of love in the moment, and it always leads to happiness.

Attitudinal Healing looks beyond words and roles by practicing forgiveness. When you see that love and happiness are inseparable, you begin to only accept roles in life that are based on love and to decline the rest. All roles that you accept where you see yourself as something other than a spiritual being will lead to inner conflict. Forgiveness will return your awareness to the truth of who you are.

Forgiveness is the means by which
you exchange all your unhappy
and fearful roles for ones that
are based on love and happiness.

Your mind comes equipped with a magnifying glass that, though you may not realize it, you use every day. This magnifying glass can bring you great joy or constant conflict, depending on your focus.

When you negatively criticize another person (or yourself) you are not seeing who they are. You are putting a magnifying glass up to mistakes instead of looking beyond them. This leads to experiencing anger, resentment, and conflict.

Change your focus and change your life! It is that simple. Choose to hold your magnifying glass up to the heart and you will see love. Remove your focus from mistakes and errors, and you will experience the peace that comes from allowing love to exist as it is, always has been, and always will be.

Do you remember, as a kid, looking into a microscope for the first time? An entire new world came into view, a world that you never before knew existed. When you choose to magnify the heart you will have the same amazement as when you first gazed into a microscope.

As you magnify love, you will discover plenty to compliment. In contrast, if you magnify mistakes, you will find plenty to criticize or complain about. Where you put your focus is up to you.

To magnify the heart, it is important, at least for a brief interval, to let go of your future goals and your past mistakes. *To have peace of mind, use your mind's magnifying glass to look for innocence in the present moment.*

Imagine that even somebody who has done things which you find very difficult to forgive has a place within him or her that is unmarred by any past actions—maybe just a speck of light. If you have a lot of anger for this person (who may even be you) imagine that this spot of love is as small as a single cell, but it is most definitely there. Now, pull out your incredibly strong magnifying glass. Focus on this single cell of love and let it be all you look at for a time.

All of us have a choice of what to magnify: anger and fear, or forgiveness and love. When you find yourself upset in any way, it is helpful to remind yourself that you are magnifying something other than the heart. During these difficult times say to yourself, "I don't want to magnify my anger, criticism, or complaints. I want to magnify love and innocence."

This thought will keep you safe in a world where there seems to be endless obstacles to focusing on love. No matter what happens during your day, you can respond with this one thought and release yourself from all pain and misery.

Sometimes when I suggest this to people, they look at me like I am living in a fantasy world. Nothing is further from the truth. In fact, when I'm not seeing love is when I am living in illusion. By focusing on love, you are looking for something that is most definitely there. The goal isn't to pretend to see something that does not exist; it is to train your mind to look beyond the mistakes so you can see what is really there.

Rather than looking forward or back in time, look directly into the present.

> *How to find love: Look past*
> *your criticisms and complaints*
> *and straight into the heart.*

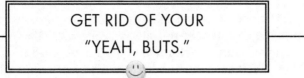

GET RID OF YOUR "YEAH, BUTS."

Many individuals throw away their peace of mind for reasons as small as a traffic jam. Resist coming up with ways by which your happiness and peace of mind can be taken away, or reasons you can't have it in the first place. Every time you have a thought like, "Well, maybe I can have peace of mind now, but if I lost my job I couldn't," you are giving up your peace of mind.

Last weekend, a septic line broke at my home, quickly filling my back yard with . . . well, I'll spare you the details. Though I can procrastinate with the best of them when it comes to home repair, I immediately called the repair people. A broken septic line is not something one puts off by saying, "Well, I have some other things to do first, I'll get to it later." On the contrary, nothing in the universe was going to take precedence over getting the flow of sewage in my back yard to stop.

Peace of mind needs to be dealt with in the same manner as a broken septic line. If I had the same commitment to peace of mind that I have to a broken septic line, I would likely be quite an enlightened soul. *Nothing can be more important in any given moment than peace of mind.*

During the 1998 International Conference for Attitudinal Healing, I met a most remarkable woman by the name of

Pilar. Her eyes were as full of light as any I have ever seen. I learned that this was not always the case. Pilar was born with no arms and a deformed body. She believed for most all of her life that she was a victim. She was angry with her mother, furious with life, and very distant from God. Consequently, she did very little with her life. Pilar felt that most people just stared at her body and wanted nothing to do with her. She felt isolated in a cruel, harsh world.

Pilar first discovered Attitudinal Healing in her home of Argentina. She was so lifted by the principles that she decided she had something to offer the world and wanted to become an artist. This made little sense to anyone, because she has no hands or arms. Nonetheless she went to college and finished with a degree in art.

Today, Pilar is a very famous artist, creating intricate and beautiful paintings using her feet. She loves life and is truly an inspiration to us all to get rid of any statements that begin with, "I could be happy, but . . . "

Take a look at your own "yeah, buts." Remind yourself that *happiness and a fulfilling life are always possible when you forgive and follow your dreams.*

Painful circumstances may be
unavoidable but suffering is optional.

9

We are students and teachers to each other.

Learning is finding out what you already know.
Doing is demonstrating that you know it.
Teaching is reminding others that they know
it just as well as you.

You are all learners, doers, teachers.

—Richard Bach

Toddlers play with such presence and truth. They smile and laugh, and when hurt, they cry and want to be held. Such simplicity. Such purity.

Tragically, in most instances, our culture begins to teach children very early to compare themselves to others in order to figure out not only how they are doing, but also *who they are.* Grades are given in school, teams are picked in sports and somebody needs to be chosen last, the "in" groups are formed.

By teenage years, models and movie stars become the standard for how we should look. Categories are created which we then use to label others and ourselves: rich and poor, smart and dumb, attractive and ugly. Innocence is lost. The message is given, "Be concerned with how you look, what you have, and what you do." For many, it never stops. Some fret with trying to figure out who they are through comparison until the very end of life, wanting to have just the right funeral—at least better than Uncle Phil's.

Attitudinal Healing recognizes that true self-esteem is never achieved by comparing yourself to others. At best, this form of comparison results in feeling superior. At worst, in feeling weak, ineffectual, powerless—a failure.

The fool's gold of the ego is believing that feelings of

superiority are self-esteem. Nothing is farther from the truth. The compulsive need to always be the best comes from fear and low self-worth. In contrast, knowing who you are, and recognizing that another person's loss is *not* your gain, brings peace to your mind and love to other beings. This is true security.

An initial step in discovering your self and realizing your connection with God is to stop asking, "How do I measure up?" Once you do this, you will start realizing we are all teachers and students to one another.

Comparison may lead to feelings of superiority, or pervasive feelings of not being good enough. Either way, comparison will eventually result in feelings of being separate and alone. This is because when we compare, we are coming from fear and are looking for outside measurements to figure out who we are.

In contrast, when we look to others as our teachers in learning to love, we experience the peace of God. A main aspect of being on a spiritual path is seeing that we are all teachers and students to each other.

By throwing away your measuring stick you begin to be able to look into your heart and to God. This is how you will know who you are.

DON'T TRY TO MAKE A ROUND PEG FIT INTO A SQUARE HOLE.

Sometimes, without even realizing it, I have tried to make other people be who *I* want them to be. When I do this, I am denying that they are my teachers.

I have also tried to make myself be somebody that I am not. I did this in hopes of making someone else happy or of getting approval. In the process, I overlooked how we could learn from each other.

It is now clear to me that if I want to be happy and have close relationships, I must begin by seeing and respecting myself and other people for who we are. Seeing us all as students and teachers to each other transforms even the most difficult relationships into classrooms in which we learn the lessons of love.

I once heard the author Ram Dass tell a story that, over time, changed how I related to people. The story was about his relationship with his brother, who was severely mentally ill. As I recall, Ram Dass would visit his brother, but would eventually become frustrated with his lack of response. His brother was clearly "in another world" and could not, or would not, connect with anybody in "this world." In order to be more peaceful, Ram Dass tried meditating before and during his visits. Nothing seemed to work. Understandably, over time, his visits became less frequent and more frustrating. One day, Ram Dass realized he was trying to make his brother enter "the world of Ram Dass" and relate according to his rules. Eventually, Ram Dass was guided to do something different . . . he entered his brother's world. In doing so, he had to suspend judgment. As you might imagine, everything changed. In these visits, Ram Dass stopped trying to make his brother be somebody he was not. He had a willingness to do his best to meet his brother where he was, without judgment and expectations. The result was a wonderful bonding.

If you want to have close relationships:

- Give up trying to make people live by your agenda.

- Try to get to know others by gaining an understanding of their world.

- Have a willingness to suspend judgment and expectations.

- See them as your teacher in opening your heart.

Another reminder of not trying to make a round peg fit into a square hole came today. As I was writing the story of Ram Dass, a case of my books arrived from the publisher. They were dropped at the top of my driveway by a delivery service. As I saw my dog Simba walk in that general direction, I ran outside—because I know Simba! I was too late to stop it, but right on time to see Simba lift his leg with what seemed to be deliberate aim. "Simba!" I yelled, as he looked back with surprise. He walked up to me as if to say, "Hey, I'm just doing what it is that I do. I'm a guy dog and guy dogs pee on anything new in the yard." He then walked away, wagging his tail—clearly joyful that he was who he was.

My whole life, animals have been my teachers. I often think my dogs are more spiritually advanced than I am! They basically live to offer unconditional affection, chase an occasional cat, wag their tails whenever my kids come down the driveway, and get a little wild under the full moon. They never try to make me into somebody I am not. In fact, they seem to know what is best about me even when I have forgotten.

In short, they appear to practice something we can all learn from:

Know what matters and don't be bothered with the rest.

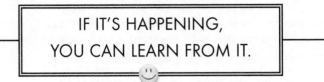

IF IT'S HAPPENING,
YOU CAN LEARN FROM IT.

We all have ideas of how we want our lives to go. If you're like most people, you won't always get what you signed up for. Because of this, many people fall into a belief system that says, "be happy when things are going well, be upset when they are not." There is another way to go through life besides having your happiness be the result of a roll of the dice.

There is a way of being in life that puts the ability to have peace of mind into the domain of *your* choice. It begins with believing that *every* situation, regardless of whether it is to your liking or not, holds the opportunity to learn of love. Quite often when I speak of this in my lectures, somebody will use the example of the holocaust, citing that certainly this would be an exception. A personal hero of mine is Viktor Frankl, a psychiatrist who went through the Holocaust. While imprisoned, he became interested in what made people survive—physically, psychologically, and spiritually. He also noted what allowed people to die peacefully. When I ask the audience what they think he found, many answer that what led to the prisoner's strength was anger and the thought that some day he would have revenge. But this is not what Frankl found. He discovered that it was the ability to love:

173

to find meaning and purpose through loving despite the horror around them. In his book *Man's Search for Meaning*, he writes:

> [We saw] the truth—that love is the ulti-
> mate and the highest goal to which man
> can aspire. . . . The salvation of man is
> through love and in love.

Even after citing this example, I have heard individuals suggest that humans are inherently flawed. They state that there never could have even been a holocaust without hate and evil. I like how Frankle speaks to this:

> After all, man is that being who has
> invented the gas chambers of Auschwitz;
> however, he is also that being who has
> entered those gas chambers upright, with
> the Lord's Prayer or the Shema Yisrael on
> his lips.

Certainly Frankl is not diminishing the horror of this time, but his experience and findings stand as a testament to the fact that *regardless of the situation, we can learn to love.* There is no goal more important than this.

"I can't be loving, I have a headache." This humorous quote illustrates the belief that if something is wrong with your body you can't be happy. Nobody wants to have their body ill or hurt. But, as thousands of people have demonstrated at the Centers for Attitudinal Healing, being sick doesn't mean not being peaceful. In fact, many people find that their illnesses can be a wakeup call to discovering what is really important to them.

Problems with your body don't need to deter you from your spiritual path. In fact, health challenges can be a road to God as much as anything else. Try to not put a label of "good" or "bad" in front of circumstances anymore. Instead just say, "Ah, this is an interesting lesson. What is there for me to learn?" Even when you find yourself upset and angry, try to pause and ask this.

I have not had a very reliable body this time around. I have had health challenges that I never expected or wanted, that have led me to having to change my life in many ways. There have certainly been times when I played the "why me?" tape, but I have found that my health challenges have led me to be able to love more fully.

> *No life is without challenges. Make them a part of learning to love fully instead of becoming reasons not to.*

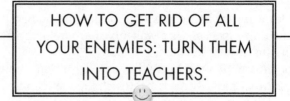

HOW TO GET RID OF ALL YOUR ENEMIES: TURN THEM INTO TEACHERS.

There was once a fellow who saw everyone around him as his enemy. His view was that his kids gave him nothing but problems, his wife was constantly cross with him, the people he worked with were a bunch of morons, and the government was even worse. He constantly complained that just about every person around him seemed to be out to get him. Finally he began praying to have a different life: Day after day, week after week, and year after year. Eventually, even God became his enemy, for why would a loving God give him such a miserable life and never answer his prayers? After he died he was complaining once again to God. Finally God said, "My son, you kept praying for a different life and I kept sending you teachers to teach you what you needed to be happy. I sent you your children to teach you understanding, patience, and perseverance. I sent you your wife to teach you how to listen with the heart. I sent you countless people to teach you how to forgive, and even more to teach you how to be of service and make a difference. In your next life, please pay attention to the teachers I send you and it will go much more smoothly than this last time around."

Think what it would be like to get up in the morning and know that the world was full of your teachers. Not one enemy, only people to help you along on your spiritual path. The guy who cuts you off on the freeway is there to teach you about letting go. The person who is late for your appointment is there to teach you about patience. Your spouse is there to teach you about kindness. Literally everyone who comes into your life is there to teach you how to see from the perspective of love and respond in compassion.

There have been times when I have tried to avoid the following spiritual truth: *Often the people who you become the most angry with are the people who have the most to teach you.* I have had resistance to this because my ego finds it much easier to be self-righteous, superior, and right than to be humble and look to all as my teachers.

If you really are honest with yourself, you probably get most upset at people for one of two reasons:

1. You see something in them you don't want to look at in yourself.

2. They are here to teach you a skill that you really need to learn but don't want to.

For example, if somebody in your life has been dishonest with you, perhaps they are here to remind you to look at the small ways in which you are dishonest. They become your teacher in forgiveness and the development of integrity.

One of the most important perceptual shifts you can make is to stop seeing enemies and start seeing teachers. This will not only allow you to be more peaceful, it will lead you to being more of the person you want to be.

> *When you stop seeing enemies and start seeing teachers, all people of the world become reflections of God. Kindness and gratitude become your response to all.*

THE WORLD IS FULL OF YOUR BROTHERS AND SISTERS.

It is not difficult to put your hand in the ocean and know that the water you touch flows through the entire sea. It is not difficult to feel the warmth of the sun upon your face and know the same rays touch all life. It is not difficult to gaze at the moon and know that its pull creates the cycles and rhythms of Earth. In the same way, look into other people and recognize that you are connected. You are of one mind, sharing the ocean of love, the warmth of the rays of compassion, the pull to turn to God.

Today, recognize your brothers and sisters. Take notice of them as you walk down the street. Smile at them in an elevator. Reach out to them in your home. Heal all conflict through seeing your common bond.

Look beyond your feelings of separation and upon the light that shines through us all.

Here is my idea of freedom: First, imagine living in your dream environment. Second, imagine living under conditions which you would not think would be to your liking. Then say, "I could be equally at peace in either place." Now that's freedom! You know that *your happiness stems from what you bring to a place, not what a place brings to you.*

That is not to say that you should not go about creating what you want for yourself: Just be careful that you don't make it the only source of your happiness. I love where I live and I feel grateful every day. Yet if unforeseen circumstances led to me need to be someplace else, I remind myself that I could be happy there, too. *Wherever I am, I can learn to love more fully, and whoever I am with can be my teacher in this.*

In contrast, to believe that you have to be in a certain situation or place to be happy is living in a kind of reverse prison—you become jailed in paradise because you fear not being there. For example, I have had several patients who were very wealthy, but lived in constant fear of losing what they had. Their affluence imprisoned them in fear. Similarly, a friend of mine recently received a large promotion. When I congratulated him he confided in me that he was depressed because he knew that he would never become an artist, something he always had wanted. He said he now was shackled with "golden handcuffs," he was making so much money in his present job that he would never be able to consider changing careers.

It is not hard to watch "Lifestyles of the Rich and Famous," and say, "I think I could be happy there." But watching the six o'clock news can be a different story. Some time ago on a road trip, I began to wonder what it would be like to randomly stop and live in any given place. These locations ranged from small farming towns, to being homeless in a large city, to mansions in the suburbs. I imagined in detail what life would be like in each spot. Then, I asked myself if I could be happy in all of these circumstances. The answer was "yes." My ego, not to be outdone, then came up with what had always been my worst nightmare: To be in prison for life for something I never did. I imagined the fear and resentment that I would have. Then a calm voice came to me and said, "If you were there, you could still go about your spiritual path. Perhaps if you were there you would be there to bring love to a place of darkness." Suddenly, I felt a freedom well up inside of me. I realized in that moment that peace ultimately has nothing to do with where you are. I imagined my worst case scenario and saw that love was still possible. This is freedom.

As my insights have the tendency to go away as quickly as they come, I decided to create a little game to serve as a reminder. It can be played alone or with others:

Drive around town, or take a road trip, and stop randomly. Look around and say, "I could be happy here."

Mean what you say. Imagine living there and deepening your spiritual path. At the end of the game, when you drive up to where you do live, say, "It is here that I am living, and I can be very happy here by choosing to love."

A place is just a place.
Home is where you choose to love.

LEARN TO SAY
"NO" GRACIOUSLY.

Smiles of calm confidence come when your thoughts, words, and actions are all in accord with each other. If your gut is saying one thing and you are doing something else, it is hard to be at peace.

For most people the word "yes" has a better ring to it than "no." *Yes* sounds smooth and is usually looked forward to. *No* sounds coarse and is generally dreaded. Typically, good news is associated with *yes,* while bad tidings begin with *no.*

In my opinion, *no* has gotten a bum rap. *No* can be just as positive as *yes,* but few people learn how to say or accept *no* in a way that leads to feelings of honor and respect.

Most of us can recall a time when we said "yes" but wanted to say "no." This happens for many different reasons, ranging from wanting to be liked, to not wanting to hurt another person's feelings, to being afraid of the consequences. Tragically, I have seen many people who have made life decisions such as marriage, having children, and in their careers because they were afraid to say a simple two-letter word.

In order to be able to say "no" graciously it is important to be able to accept "no" without seeing it as something negative. What helps me with this is looking at what my life would have been like if I had received a "yes" every time I thought I wanted one. The truth is, many of the yes-responses I wanted wouldn't have been so great for my life at the time.

Sometimes we can be like teenagers, thinking that we know everything when we really have no clue. In this frame of mind, we can get quite upset at the word no, rather than looking at the overall situation in the larger context of our life.

In the bigger picture, I believe that there is a wisdom which runs through our lives. Sometimes this wisdom brings a "no" to us because that is the best thing, even though we cannot see it. I like to think of this wisdom as a wise parent, or even a guardian angel. The next time you hear "no", imagine that there is a benevolent energy helping you along on your spiritual path.

When I submit books for publication, it is very possible that I will receive rejection letters. A saying that is helpful for me is, "Every 'no' means you are that much closer to 'yes.'" On my spiritual, path I like to change this saying slightly to, "Every 'no' and every 'yes' bring me that much closer to God."

In order to accept "no" graciously, remind yourself of the following:

- There is a wisdom to life that you can trust.

- The person who is saying "no" is offering you an opportunity that you don't know about yet.

- A "no" is like brussels sprouts—good for
  you but not too tasty. Rest assured,
  dessert is on its way.

If you adopt these beliefs, it also becomes much easier to say "no." If you are following your inner guidance, there is not a reason to feel guilty or a need to apologize for saying "no." To the contrary, if someone asks you something and you turn within to your own inner wisdom for the answer, you are doing both of you a service.

A few years ago I asked a friend of mine, Anita Whitaker, a favor. It was hard for me to ask her because what I wanted was both important and a bit embarrassing. She said "no." But how she said it left me feeling very cared about. Here is what she said: "I am so glad you thought enough of me and our friendship to ask. What you asked me is not something I choose to do right now. However, I would really like the opportunity to help you with something else in the future, so please ask me again."

Despite hearing a "no," I felt genuinely cared about. If she had said "yes," but really didn't want to, there is no way I would have felt as good. Her response included three key points that are important in saying "no" graciously:

1. Acknowledge the worth of the person and
   your relationship with them.

2. State a clear "no." Don't be wishy-washy.

3. Make a positive statement about the future.

Learning to say and accept "no" is an important part of the spiritual journey. It is a demonstration of trust and faith.

Follow your intuition and speak the truth. Encourage the intuition of other people and respect their truth. This is friendship.

10

We can focus on the whole of life rather than the fragments.

I know not with what weapons World War III will be fought, but World War IV will be fought with sticks and stones.

—Albert Einstein

I want to know God's thoughts . . . all the rest are just details.

—Albert Einstein

DEVELOP INTENTION,
LET GO OF PERFECTION.

Traveling through India with Mother Teresa, I was having an increasingly difficult time with all of the hunger, pain, and illness I saw. My energy was depleted and I felt depressed. Mother Teresa, on the other hand, was full of life and remained loving and present.

Because I was focusing on the fragments of the situation, my response to poverty was hopelessness and helplessness. Mother Teresa's response to *the same* situation was the extension of loving kindness. This is because she was clearly focusing on the whole of life with God as her guide.

I asked her how she did it. Her simple words have greatly influenced my life. *"Have the intention to be as loving as you can and ask for God's help."* I believe all spirituality is held in this simple phrase. What else could there possibly be to happiness?

Whenever you become confused or find yourself struggling, remember to direct your mind in two ways:

1. Have clear intentions.

2. Ask for God's help.

Your intentions set the direction in which you wish your life to go. Asking for God's help allows you to not be sidetracked.

When you know you want to be
loving, and you ask for God's help,
there is no obstacle you can't overcome.

WE CAN FOCUS ON THE WHOLE OF LIFE RATHER THAN THE FRAGMENTS.

189

Have you ever noticed which branches of a tree are the first to break in a strong wind? The branches that are supple and able to bend with the wind are able to survive, while those that are rigid snap, though often they appear the strongest.

How you respond to stress and change is imperative to your peace of mind. Despite how strong you might appear, if you are unwilling to listen, compromise, or change you will likely be doing a great deal of "snapping." In contrast, being able to bend in the inevitable winds of life leads to calm and happiness.

You become stiff and inflexible by having narrow vision, a closed mind, and focusing on the little, fragmented pieces of life. The more you do this the more you lose the ability to see from a larger and more peaceful perspective.

The ego's faulty logic tells you that if you take care of all the little stuff you will be less stressed. When you feel overwhelmed, this approach can make sense. The problem is that *the more you focus upon the little stuff, ignoring the larger truths to life, the higher your stress level goes*. This does *not* mean to just ignore all the details and problems of your life and try to be blissful. Rather, don't overlook God and the whole of your life as you go about your daily activities.

The ego wants to solve problems by separating everything into little pieces: money, relationship, work, family. In the process, it forgets about the whole and the higher purposes of life—such as giving and receiving love.

There is an old story of two blind men describing an elephant. One is feeling the tail, the other the trunk. Neither of them describes the entire elephant, believing instead that their little piece is the whole animal. Similarly, it is easy to miss the meaning of your life when you focus on the small fragments.

The five most common ways of focusing on the fragments are by becoming overly concerned with:

1. What somebody did or said in the past.

2. Lack of reciprocation.

3. Mistakes.

4. Your body.

5. Money.

Think about how much time you spend on these concerns. They have no ability in themselves to determine your happiness—it is only your over-focusing upon them that deprives you of peace.

If you step back and remind yourself that there is something beyond the fragments your stress will begin to dissipate, automatically and immediately. This is because as you broaden your focus you will see the whole of life, which is always love.

When I am upset about something, one question that helps me to step back is, "Will this matter to me five years from now?" To fully answer the question I have to broaden my vision, focus on the whole, and thus recognize what is really important.

There are ways of directing your mind that will lead you to seeing the whole. I call these "Doorways to Truth." The five primary doorways are:

1. Look for love in the present moment.

2. Know all minds are joined and want love.

3. Forgive.

4. See opportunities to learn in all circumstances.

5. Recognize the abundance of all that is important.

The narrow-thinking mind hides the power of all you are from your awareness.

YOUR LIFE IS NOT AN AUDITION FOR A SOAP OPERA.

One day I looked at my daily activities and realized how much thought and energy was going into the various soap operas being played out in my life. Drama was everywhere. When I went to sleep at night, my thoughts sounded like the closing minutes of a daytime soap.

In conversation with friends, I found the drama of our lives was receiving more attention than the joys and pleasures. It was like having a garden full of flowers that was overgrown by weeds—and the weeds received the water.

I decided I didn't want to overlook the flowers anymore. This does not mean that I wanted to ignore the situations in my life which needed attention. Simply put, I wanted to devote my life to peace and happiness and not create any unnecessary drama. I have found many role models in doing so—people who are spiritually centered and involve themselves in the world through compassionate acts, but don't get hooked into drama.

It is not easy to follow a spiritual path in our culture when there is so much juicy drama everywhere. In case you don't have enough drama in your own life, there are now numerous television shows which offer live action of other people's drama. Don't take the bait. Spend time emptying your mind of drama, not filling it back up.

The ego's sole need for drama is to help it deter you from the peace of God. You may have noticed that it is not easy to quiet your mind. This is because the ego has a direction it always tries to follow: Insert drama into any open and quiet space. The way out of this is to remind yourself that drama comes from focusing on the fragments of life, while peace comes from focusing on the whole.

You have a choice: You can involve yourself in drama or you can turn to God. This one decision can simplify life tremendously.

DON'T PUT ROCKS IN
YOUR KNAPSACK.

Sitting on Monterey Beach on an early spring day, dogs and children playing happily in the ocean, I saw a large sailboat that the last El Niño storm broke loose from its mooring. The vessel had lodged itself deep in the sand, waves breaking over her stern. To no avail, a team of salvagers tried move her. Her hull was full of thick, wet sand. She was too heavy for three tow trucks to pull to the beach, or the tugboat to pull back to the sea.

With the offshore breeze, smelling of seaweed and salt water, I began thinking of a newspaper story I read earlier. It described the quandary of some ducks.

Upon their usual migratory flight, they stopped at an island off the coast of California. There, they feasted upon the unusually abundant small red crabs. Apparently, a duck-dining delicacy, they ate so many they could no longer fly. Their wings flapped feverishly, but they could not ascend. Apparently unaware of what caused their problem, they continued to eat.

These stories—the beached boat and the land-bound ducks—illustrate what happens when you weigh yourself down and become stuck or trapped. In the storms of life, you can break away from what keeps you from drifting into dangerous waters: your spiritual path. Without a spiritual path you become so heavy with shame, blame, guilt, stress, and endless problems that you believe you cannot be set afloat or "salvaged." You sit, taking on water (more problems), listing from side to side, waiting for the final wave that will break you.

And as for the birds, reflect on how many times our desires seem to fill our stomachs but keep us from flying—and we keep on eating.

A simple and quick way to keep light and on track spiritually is to remind yourself of the one thing that will never change in this life, regardless of what you have or don't have, do or don't do:

You are something much larger than all the fragments that you burden yourself with. You are a child of God. *When you know this there is nothing that can weigh you down.*

KNOW WHAT'S ENOUGH.

You are, no doubt, quite familiar with the nagging voice in your head that keeps the pressure on by saying things like: "Take on more. Accomplish more. Get more done in less time. Make more money. Buy more and better possessions."

Of all the things you can know, knowing what is enough is one of the most important. This knowledge is the core of a simple life. It comes from looking at the whole of life rather than the fragments. In contrast, always wanting more, bigger, and better will take you on an endless and relentless treadmill, leading you away from the simple knowledge of what is enough. In the process of accomplishing and acquiring, without asking yourself what is enough, you lose sight of what is important.

Until you learn to recognize what is enough, nothing will give you true or lasting satisfaction. When you are on the treadmill, you will likely delude yourself into thinking that you will soon have time for what is important. But the time never comes because you don't ask yourself three words, "What is enough?"

You have probably bought items of technology believing they would give you more time for what is important. Did fax machines give you more time at home? Did e-mail give you more time to yourself for contemplation? Did the Internet offer you extra free time? Of course this is not the fault of technology, rather it is a result of your thinking. Technology, like anything else, can be a tool to free you or imprison you. If you have a "take on more" mentality, you will find ways to take on more. If you have a "know what is enough" focus, you will have time in your life for what is important. With this you will use technology and other means to support you in having enough.

Pay attention to what is enough by looking to the whole of life. This is essentially what spirituality is, and it is the source of simplicity.

WATCH YOUR LANGUAGE.

In 1984, while living in Mexico, I attended a language school. In the process of learning a new vocabulary, I became aware of the words that limit happiness, negatively judge, or label. I found that I had the unique opportunity to choose to *not* learn certain words.

Simply put, words can help set you free or keep you stuck in unhappiness. More specifically:

Language is the structure of your thoughts.

Your thoughts create your experience.

Therefore, the words you use can shape your life.

"Limiting words" are ones which describe you or another person as anything other than a spiritual being in a limit-less moment—words such as can't, impossible, and never. "Judging words" are ones which keep unforgiving thoughts going—words such as inferior, stupid, and weak. "Labeling words" are ones which categorize or pigeonhole in a way that holds an individual or group back from all they can be—words such as hopeless, useless, or any words used in a racist manner.

When you choose to stop using words which limit, judge, or label, your life becomes more peaceful. Without the negative words, it is hard to have the negative thoughts, and in their place you discover more compassionate and loving thoughts. I like to think of this as "word surgery." If there were something toxic in your body, surely you would want it removed to allow the body to flourish in its state of health. Similarly, by not using limiting, judging, or labeling words, you allow your mind to return to its natural state of love. If these words do come up in your thinking, try to stop and see that you must be entertaining a false belief about yourself or another person, and your thinking has become toxic. Remove the words and allow your mind to return to love.

Try the following ten-minute experiment to demonstrate the power of words. In the first five minutes repeat the following five words to yourself:

Hate, Impossible, Afraid, Frown, Separate.

Note how you feel: Probably pretty yucky. In the next five minutes repeat the following five words to yourself:

Forgive, Possible, Love, Smile, One.

Note how you feel: Probably pretty wonderful! All from just thinking a few words. This gives you good reason to *watch your language*.

You have surely been asked questions like, "If you could

only have one food for the rest of your life, what would it be?" Ask your self the similar type of question, "If you could only have one word for the rest of your life what would it be?" Mine would be *love*.

> *Let love be the source of all*
> *your thoughts, all your words,*
> *and all your actions.*

A friend and colleague of mine has many framed certificates and diplomas prominently displayed on his office wall. To be honest, I always thought it a bit pretentious. It also seemed out of character for my friend. He always seemed so full of spontaneity and enthusiasm, not the sort of person who would rely heavily on his accomplishments to get respect from people. One day, while I was waiting for a meeting with him in his office, I took a closer look at his wall display. I let out a belly laugh that he heard as he was walking in the front door.

"Hey, do I sit alone in your office and laugh?" he ribbed. "Exactly what is it that you find so funny?"

"In all the years I have known you, I never looked closely at your wall of diplomas," I replied.

My friend smiled, knowing that as I read the framed papers I was laughing as much at my own assumptions as his sense of humor. What I found on his wall was that of the eight frames only two held anything of his. The rest were for his dog; fancy looking diplomas from obedience school.

Being attached to accomplishments can be detrimental to peace of mind. Fred, a patient I saw many years ago, was a forty-three year old high school teacher. He had built a life around teaching, had an excellent reputation, and had won several awards. The problem was that he secretly had increasing anxiety everyday he went to work. He knew that he helped his students, but he had never really loved teaching. His anxiety increased every year until he could not deny it any longer.

Fred discovered that his accomplishments were vast, his profession respectable, but he was not doing what he felt he was guided to do. For many years, he had been able to get rid of these thoughts by telling himself he was too broke to do anything else and that he was good at what he was doing. Then he began telling himself he was too old.

In his work with me, he began to allow himself to ask his inner wisdom for guidance on his life path. As he did so, the anxiety began to cease. At forty-four he was accepted to graduate school in psychology. The last I heard, he was a doctor working with AIDS patients and their families, and feeling very fulfilled.

In order to find your true passion, you need to be willing to release your old accomplishments and look to the whole of your life. Be proud of what you have done, but don't let the fragments of your life determine your future. Resist defining yourself by what you were (even if it is impressive), and allow yourself to see yourself as who you are.

*The ability to let go of what
you accomplish is far more useful
than the accomplishment itself.*

LOOK FOR WHAT IS RIGHT AND KNOW THERE IS NOTHING MISSING.

The part of your mind that is fearful will always look at fragments to find what is wrong, believing that doing so will keep you from making mistakes in your life. The problem with this way of thinking is that it overlooks the fact that all of your thoughts create. This means that if you focus too much on what is wrong, what is lacking, or what might go wrong in the future, this is what you are "priming" your mind for.

Though we have never met, I can tell you something about yourself: *There is nothing missing in your heart and there is nothing wrong with you.* There is nothing missing because, at a deep level, you are connected with all that is. There is nothing wrong with you because you are still as God created you. In this moment, there is nothing absent from your life that keeps you from experiencing a rich and consistent peace. What you may think is missing (fragments such as money, a relationship, youth, better health) are really things that, somewhere along the line, you decided were valuable, and their absence has led you to feel, like something is missing.

Many missed opportunities are created every day because of looking for what is wrong with other people, a certain opportunity, or ourselves. It is indeed sad that so many people keep themselves from wonderful and meaningful relationships, successful careers, and new opportunities because their minds are so accustomed to thinking that safety lies in figuring out what is wrong with their life.

The alternative is to train your mind to focus on what is right. The fearful part of your mind may emphatically state that this will surely lead to disaster because you will end up in a bad situation by overlooking what is wrong. I assure you that this is unlikely to occur. In the same way an animal knows what to eat and what not to eat, you intuitively know what is right for you. You may have become distant from this knowledge, but it still exists within you. Nevertheless, give yourself some room to get used to the idea, and decide *not* to make any large changes right away. Simply see how you feel when you direct your mind to what is right.

Focusing on what is right is most important in your relationships. For example, many parents believe they are being helpful by offering constant "constructive criticism," but may forget to tell their children what they see as wonderful and right about them. Further, many spouses become acclimated to focusing on what bothers them about their partner and forget to see and communicate what they appreciate. Many new relationships never even begin because, upon meeting somebody, people focus on the differences instead of the commonalties.

Focus on what is right by practicing the following:

Think about what is right in your life. Think about what is right with your body. If any of this is difficult for you, begin with the miracles of life . . . the beating of your heart, the vision your eyes offer, your ability to hear the wind in the trees, how you can smell wildflowers in the spring, and taste the tartness of freshly-squeezed juice.

Think about the people in your life, and what is right about them. If you are tempted to be critical, choose instead to rejoice in their humanity. If feasible, contact them and let them know everything that you see as right in them.

If you spend your life focusing on what is wrong and what is missing, your life will likely be filled with the experience of lack, frustration, and despair. Instead:

Look for what is right and beautiful. It is always there for you to find.

11

Since love is eternal, death need not be viewed as fearful.

If you spend your life overly concerned with just the temporary affairs of this lifetime, and make no preparation for it [death], then on the day when it comes you will be unable to think about anything except your own mental suffering and fear, and will have no opportunity to practice anything else.

The Dalai Lama,
in *Kindness, Clarity, and Insight*

It is not that I am afraid to die. I just don't want to be there when it happens.

Woody Allen

A major contributor to unhappiness is confusion about what is valuable. One reason people have a difficult time with life, as well as with death, is that they have lost sight of what is valuable. Those who believe wholeheartedly that love is eternal, and is the source of all that has any value, have every reason to enjoy life and no reason to fear death.

Modern culture has made huge advances in many areas, which have led to a higher standard of living. Along with this have also come some problems. It is not hard to get confused in your values when you are exposed to a fast-paced and materialistic culture. You can be the passive recipient of countless advertisements in any given day. All are communicating basically the same message: "Something outside of yourself will make you feel happier."

Because of this cultural influence, it is important to periodically take some time and ask yourself the question, "Where is it that my happiness really comes from?" This is an important question because where you think your happiness comes from will determine what you value and what you pursue.

If you value what is valueless, you will end up scared in some way. This is because that which is valueless will not last forever. Thus you will fear its loss. Because what is valuable is eternal there is no need to fear loss.

If you attach too much value to something that is valueless you will become overly attached, and it will begin to own you. Look around. You can find many people who are behaving as though they can't live without something. They forget that they gave it all the value that it has for them. In Western culture, it is easy to believe that the more possessions you have, the happier you will be. In contrast, there are cultures which don't even have a word for ownership.

There are three questions to ask yourself to determine if something is valuable:

1. Will what I value last forever?
Time can never diminish that which has true value. The gifts of love, compassion, and tenderness do not rust or fade. In fact, they grow the more they are given.

2. Will pursuing what I value lead to loss for anyone?
When you seek to take something away from another person or harm them, you have made the mistake of thinking that another person's loss can be your gain.

3. Will what I value bring peace to others and myself?
Most material things can be vehicles of love and service or vehicles for greed, fear, and control. Material possessions are what we make of them.

There are many examples of people who have lost their homes, even their homeland, who have gone on to be happy and giving people. There are also examples of those who never get over the loss and remain bitter. The difference is in what is valued. If you always see love as the highest of values, you will always, eventually, land on your feet with a smile on your face.

Be a philanthropist. Determine what is most valuable (love) and then give it away lavishly.

The wife of a friend of mine has a license plate which reads: "QOE." When I asked my friend what it meant, he smiled and said, "Why, 'Queen of Everything,' of course!" Her license plate humorously reminds us to be humble and know that we can only play at being the boss of the universe.

In contrast, and not so humorously, many people don't know they are playing a dangerous game when they see themselves as the boss of the universe. Modern humans, especially the Western male, have shown the unfortunate tendency to think that we can dominate the environment with no consequences. Wrong.

Having reverence and appreciation for being part of one humanity can be lost in the fast pace of the world. Slow down and be humbled. It is essential to happiness, and to our planetary survival, to realize that controlling other people and dominating the environment will not lead to peace of mind.

One central attitude that comes from being humble is respect: respect for life, respect for the environment, and respect for the challenges in life that allow you to grow. It is our disowned fear that leads to the desire to dominate and control.

Think about what people look like when they want to control and dominate. They don't smile much. It doesn't matter how successful they are at the domination game, they still don't look very happy. On the other hand, think about somebody you know who is truly humble. Or choose someone like the Dalai Lama or other spiritual figures who practice humility. Just looking at them gives you a sense of peace! They have something that you and I can also reach—humility.

There are two common misconceptions about humility. First, some people mistakenly see humility as a result of comparing yourself to another person and discovering that you are less than in some way. Second, it is a common mistake to see humility a result of seeing something much larger or more extraordinary than yourself and being "humbled" by comparison.

> It is true that humility comes from seeing the magnificence of love and life, but it results from knowing you are *a part of it* not *apart from it.* When you stand in awe of something, remind yourself that you share the source from which it came.

Humility is an attitude based on abundance and the knowledge that the power of love is available to you at all times. Humility doesn't come from comparison, but rather from recognizing the shared source of life and the miracle within life and nature. Humility is recognizing that there is no one life "better" than another and that all life is precious. This is why respect and kindness are natural extensions of humility.

With fear and control you become blind to the interconnectedness of life. With humility you gain vision into all that love is.

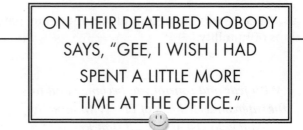

ON THEIR DEATHBED NOBODY
SAYS, "GEE, I WISH I HAD
SPENT A LITTLE MORE
TIME AT THE OFFICE."

What many people do say on their deathbed is, "I wish I had spent more time loving those around me." It is ironic that we can yearn for what we have available to us at all times. But because of our egos, this can be the case.

Innumerable people spend most of their lives getting things done which *seem* important, but they lose sight of what is *really* important. When the end comes, they have regrets. They wish they had lived a more balanced life. A painful discovery is often made through the process of dying: Without love, even the most momentous life achievement is empty. It is no wonder that those who have come close to dying almost always describe it as a positive, life-changing experience. They come out of it with a deep sense of what is important and what doesn't really matter.

If you knew that your time was limited, how would you want to live your life today, this month, and this year? For most of us, the answer includes loving more deeply, expressively, completely, and consistently. When we think of our time as limited, our thoughts seem to automatically go to what is important rather than the trivial.

Your time in this life *is* limited, so begin living your days knowing that each of them is a precious gift. The finite nature of this existence is something that is often overlooked because death is feared. Death is often hidden from view because nobody wants to be reminded of the end.

An alternative to the fear and denial of death is to see that you are here for one purpose, to give and receive love, and that this love is eternal. Tremendous peace comes with the recognition of your purpose and that love lives beyond the end of your body's existence.

Satisfying work, personal strength, and successful, intimate relationships can be the exception rather than the rule. This is because we have forgotten what their source is. Imagine someone exerting great effort to push a car that has run out of fuel. Despite being right next to a gas station the stranded driver still pushes, complains, and struggles. This is the case with many of our lives. We struggle instead of taking the time to pause and give and receive love, even though this is precisely what will make our lives run smoothly.

A love-centered life is certainly not a new idea, but it is a much needed one. Love does not promise a pain- and trouble-free life, but it does offer one of tremendous peace, depth, and meaning. Love is not to be figured out or understood with the mind: It is to be experienced with the heart.

Love now. There is literally no time like the present.

A HEARSE DOESN'T HAVE A TRAILER HITCH.

·‿·

Jonathan was dying. He knew he was, and he had called together his family to discuss his wishes after his death. His brother was carefully asking about the funeral arrangements and choices to be made. Jonathan responded with his usual humor, significantly lightening the mood, "Who cares about the color of the casket, I want to know how big a trailer I can have!"

If you look around you, there are likely to be many people believing in the misguided philosophy that whoever has the most possessions upon departing this world is the most successful. Today there is an excessive quest for material wealth, sexual fulfillment, and entertainment. These pursuits serve as a distraction to pervasive feelings of emptiness, disillusionment, misplaced values, purposelessness, and unrecognized spiritual thirst. It is time to return to the love of the heart and to the soul.

We have all heard, "You can't take it with you." Though this suggests a reality about material possessions, it fails to address spiritual development. There is in fact a great deal you can take with you, but it is not what you may have spent your life accumulating; things such as money, prestige, and job success.

This is not to say that in order to be spiritual, one needs

to become a homeless wanderer with no possessions. There is nothing inherently wrong with material comfort. It is your attachment to it that creates problems. In short, the pitfalls of materialism come primarily from two ways of being:

- You believe your happiness is dependent on having, keeping, or acquiring something.

- You use possessions and money as a means to distract yourself from your inner challenges and spiritual journey.

The alternative to materialism is to realize that you are blessed in every moment by giving and receiving love, kindness, and compassion. These are eternal. However, the cultivation and experience of these qualities is rarely without pain. I know of no person who has experienced a life without challenges. Materialism can appear to offer a very simple and direct solution to emotional and spiritual discomfort: Gain possessions and prestige and you will be happy. The inner path of spirituality is more subtle because at the center is seeking purpose and sacredness in the mystery of each individual life.

If you follow the illusory path to happiness that materialism promises, you will most certainly be disappointed. This is because you will be worshipping a god that will take all away in the end, leaving you with the emptiness you feared all along. However, in order to have a spiritual path, it is not enough to simply cease being overly materialistic, though realizing the pitfalls of being so is essential. The positive alternative to the pursuit of materialism is to turn inward. Look toward the center of your being, where there is a deep and unfathomable mystery. Following the path to this mystery is not always easy, but will always bring you to a deeper experience of the essence of love and service.

Love is both the mystery and the guide through the mystery. To distract yourself from it is to miss the greatest of journeys.

While watching the movie *Titanic,* and later *Life Is Beautiful,* I was struck by varying attitudes and actions that people had while facing their death. Some were frantic, terrified, and screaming, but these were not what intrigued me. Those who were compassionate, thoughtful, and peaceful captured my attention as they approached the last moments of their life.

A scene from *Titanic* beckoned to the part of myself that knows I will one day be facing my own death, and will have a choice of what I will be thinking when I die. As the ship was sinking, three musicians in their formalwear looked about the chaos of struggle and death. They glanced into each other's eyes and made a silent collective choice. They began to passionately play their music, for themselves and others, while the ship went down. They chose to die while giving their gift. What class! A moment like that tells what a person's life was about: no biography needed beyond that single choice.

Similarly, in the Academy Award winning Italian film, *Life Is Beautiful,* one discovers the depths love can bring to the most desperate of situations. In the horror of a Nazi concentration camp, love is discovered to transcend all. In the last moments of his life, a father loves his son beyond measure. As a result, purpose, hope, and beauty radiate in the midst of atrocity, suffering, and useless death.

These films bring me to ask the question, "When it is my time, with what thoughts, attitudes, and actions do I want to die?" The answer brings me to how I want to live today.

The experience of love is not in a book or classroom. It lives in your heart, waiting for a simple invitation asked with sincerity.

My father is fond of saying, "If I were to discover a pill that, with absolutely no side affects, would guarantee you peace, reduced stress, better health, close relationships, and increased vitality it would be a miracle! There is such a miracle, it is called forgiveness!"

When I have suffered in my life it has been from lack of forgiveness. Similarly, I have witnessed patients grieving the death of somebody whom they had not forgiven. Often, their grief stems from wishing they had communicated a few words like, "I love you."

There is a problem with being so angry at somebody that you want them to take their guilt to the grave: Until you forgive, *you* carry guilt through your life. You might like to believe that your anger and upset will vanish when somebody dies, but it is not true. It is with your own thoughts which you must work, and it is never too late to practice forgiveness. The opportunity to forgive isn't withdrawn at the time of death.

I have encountered numerous individuals who so wished they had dealt with an unhealed relationship before their own death was upon them. Things look quite different when you know you are soon to depart. Like the first time one flies in an airplane, looking down and seeing how small everything looks, death brings with it the perspective that all the anger and unforgiving thoughts are quite small, trivial, and insignificant. It makes sense to strive to see this while you are still alive and kicking.

Many relationships are plagued by a lack of shared feelings. Part of physical, emotional, and spiritual health is being able to experience and communicate your feelings. Unfortunately, many people rarely, if ever, communicate how they feel. Countless people develop physical illness from having anger, loneliness, and guilt attack their bodies. Many others never have emotional intimacy because of unexpressed feelings. So much suffering results from not talking honestly from the heart.

Think about the people in your life. If they were not here any longer, or if you were soon to depart, is there something you would have wished you had said or hoped they would have known? Tell them today!

When you see today for all it holds, and all it doesn't have to, you start to live.

With all life's flash and glitz, it is easy to lose appreciation for the ordinary, the simple things in life. Technology has great potential to bring us together, and share, but if you drift too far from the grounding of nature, people, and love you will become lost.

Within the ordinary occurrences of nature the path to the sacred is found: the scent of pine in the forest, your bare feet upon sun drenched white sand, an expanse of green grass blowing in a summer breeze as you lean back to watch wisps of white clouds dance across the sky, looking out your window to see the stars sparkling across the expanse of the universe.

Time with nature brings balance. Without it, your life path can become shallow, even dangerous. With it, you stay connected to your source.

I would rather see fewer prescriptions for Valium and Prozac and more for turning to nature. Many years ago, I found myself doing well in my career, but I was not feeling a strong sense of purpose or meaning in my life. I backpacked into the Sierra Nevada Mountains, knowing that being in nature was somehow important. After a few days,

I discovered a renewed sense of purpose to my life, purely by being close to nature. If you asked me to put my experience in words I don't think I could – it is more of a feeling, a knowing. Many times in my life I have embarked on similar journeys, sometimes only for a few hours. I have never entered nature with the purpose of finding grounding and balance and come up short.

Too much time away from nature and you forget that you are part of a quiet rhythm. Allow nature to soften your soul and heal your heart.

12

We can always perceive ourselves and others as either extending love or giving a call for help.

I define love thus: The will to extend one's self for the purpose of nurturing one's own or another's spiritual growth.

. . . Whenever we do actually exert ourselves in the cause of spiritual growth, it is because we have chosen to do so. The choice to love has been made.

M. Scott Peck
in *The Road Less Traveled*

I can't think of anything that patience doesn't improve. It is like angels left something for us mortals to use. Every time somebody has been patient with me there is instant bonding and appreciation in my heart, even if I was not able to show it.

Patience is always an extension of love, and therefore always is of benefit. If someone is having a difficult time, getting upset, judging, or pressuring may get some type of result, but they will never improve the quality of the relationship. However, if you respond with patience, the situation takes on a different energy and feeling.

The best way to shift a situation from a problematic struggle to a positive communication is to stop judging and see the person as making a call for help—for love. Remember, calls for help are not always straightforward. Sometimes the ugliest of behavior from another person is really a call for help. No matter what they are saying or doing, think of a subtitle flashing across their heart saying, "The reason I am behaving this way is that I feel afraid and alone. What I really want is to be loved."

Although patience is something we give other people, as with all acts of love, we are equal recipients of the gift. Patience directly teaches that to give is to receive. The simplest reason to be patient is that it feels a whole lot better than being a controlling, stressed-out maniac. When you make the choice to develop patience, you take a tremendous weight off of your shoulders. Then your heart naturally opens.

When you become uptight, or try to force something to happen according to *your* time, it is because you are untrusting of the outcome. This is where a spiritual focus can change your life. For example, if you know that the most important thing to do is to extend love, and you trust in the outcome when love is the guide, then you can wait without anxiety. So, it can be said that to be patient is to trust in the power of love.

Another way of saying this is that you become impatient when you are afraid. You end up trying to control (which you are doing whenever you are not being patient) when you fear that the future won't be how you think it should be, or when you fear the past will repeat itself.

Speed seems to be a hot commodity today. *Faster* is what sells: faster people, faster computers, and faster travel. If a discussion takes more than a sound bite it seems too long.

In contrast, I have yet to see the word "speed" in conjunction with any true spiritual practice. Something miraculous happens when you decide to be patient. Patience opens the door to the magic of the moment, where lessons of love abound and anything is possible.

Fear and impatience are inseparable. Patience comes when you trust in the power of God's Love.

Are you busy but without purpose? Are you reluctant to make decisions or changes because you are afraid you will make a mistake or fail? If the answer is "yes" to either question, you are not alone. Many people have a block in the natural cycle of awareness, trust, and action.

Though it is typically not difficult for me to make decisions, earlier today I took at least three hours to make a relatively simple one. I made the whole thing into quite a big deal. Instead of paying attention to what I knew to be true, I became way too involved in my head. I weighed the alternatives, I thought of which decision was best for other people, I considered time constraints, I tried to predict the outcome of all alternatives, I prayed (as well as can be done when I am stuck in my intellect), and I talked. I exhausted myself. Finally, I made a decision. Then I changed my mind. At last, I laughed at how far from simple wisdom I can wander.

It is difficult to see the truth about a situation, or to know how to react, when you are wringing out your mind like a wet towel.

In my work with animals, especially herd animals such as horses, I have noticed that they're always aware. There is a sensitivity to their surroundings, to the life in and around them, and to what action is needed. There is absolutely nothing dishonest about them. Their actions come from being aware of, and trusting in, a natural wisdom. They don't say, as I did earlier today, "Well, a part of me feels this way, and part of me feels the other way." Based on their awareness, and trusting in the information that comes from that awareness, they take action. There is no, "Am I making the right decision." There is no, "I need more information." There is no, "Can you give me more time."

In response to my observations on the wisdom of animals it has been said to me, "Well, humans have a cerebral cortex that differentiates us from animals. With it, we can think and reason." I reply, "As with any advanced technology, it is good to know how and when to turn the thing off." Reason and other "higher" brain functions can be wonderful tools, but they can also be slippery partners. Sometimes, if not most times, we are way too much in our heads. To make good decisions and take appropriate actions, take time each day to ask yourself the following:

What am I aware of?

Use your five senses, plus be aware of your soul and your connection with all that is.

What am I feeling in my heart?

Many times, the answers of the heart are beyond words, and come via a "sense of knowing." God speaks to you through your heart, but not always in words.

What action(s) am I guided to take?

Here is where you may have to stretch. It is one thing to listen to guidance, but it takes guts to follow it. Change occurs whether you want it or not, so you might as well try following your inner guidance. In doing so, change becomes your friend because you come to know the one aspect of life that never changes: God's Love for you.

Be aware of all you are. Trust who speaks to you through your heart. Take loving actions, and know you do not walk alone.

DO SMALL ACTS OF KINDNESS AND YOUR BIG PROBLEMS WON'T BE SO BIG.

A rule I have noticed in life is: *People with many big problems don't do very many small acts of kindness.* Little acts of compassion don't seem to be a part of their life, like stopping for kids to cross the street and smiling at them, or helping a neighbor with a project.

However, *people who do small acts of kindness from the heart don't have many big problems.* When problems do arise, they don't seem to be quite as insurmountable.

My father told me the following story. There had been a hurricane in Hawaii that devastated many of the beaches and sea life. In one spot, hundreds of starfish were strewn across the sand. A man in his early fifties was slowly walking along the beach, picking up single starfish and carrying them to the sea. A younger man approached him and suggested that he not waste his time, saying his efforts would not make a difference to such large devastation. As the older man placed another starfish into the sea he said to the younger man, "Made a difference to that one."

In every act of kindness, there is the seed of healing the world and ourselves. Every small act of kindness brings purpose and meaning to the moment. Attitudinal Healing

WE CAN ALWAYS PERCEIVE OURSELVES AND OTHERS AS EXTENDING LOVE OR GIVING A CALL FOR HELP.

235

recognizes that *as we heal, we are healed, as we give, so shall we receive*. Every moment affords you the opportunity to do this, even when you have big problems.

> *The best way to get rid of a life of big problems is to practice small acts of kindness.*

LEARN TO BE
WITH YOURSELF.

Many people are so busy attending to the details of their life that they don't know how to be with themselves. With so much to do, and with so little time to oneself, spiritual thirst often goes unrecognized for what it is. Depression, anxiety, and boredom can be symptoms of an unanswered call to a spiritual path.

I have found the things people say they want the most are: positive relationships, good health, and personal power and self-esteem. There is a great deal of time and money spent pursuing them. Unfortunately the most important and natural first step to achieving these is often overlooked: Spending reflective time with yourself.

Conflicted relationships, low self-esteem, and lack of peace of mind are all indicators that you need to be spending contemplative time with yourself. Yet, often, people don't do this because they believe they should be spending all their time fixing problems.

You cannot be powerful and be afraid of who you are. When you are afraid, the most you can do is control. Though many have come to believe that this is power, it is not. Authentic power comes from knowing your connection with all that is. When you spend reflective time with yourself you discover this power.

Power is knowing that God loves you. This knowledge will change your whole world. That is not to say that knowing yourself and your connection with God releases you from the challenges and pains of living, but it does give you an anchor and a compass during the storms. The anchor is faith and the compass is hope.

Hope and faith help us to envision a positive outcome, even during trying times. I know of nobody with strong hope and faith who does not spend time with himself in reflection, prayer, and meditation. *A positive life comes from having hope and faith, and hope and faith come from spending reflective time with yourself.*

> *The first person to spend quality time with is yourself, in quiet, with God. This is the foundation and source of all else that you want.*

> CHOOSE ONE PERSON YOU
> KNOW, ONE PERSON YOU
> DON'T, AND DO SOMETHING
> KIND FOR THEM . . . AND DON'T
> LET THEM KNOW IT WAS YOU.

☺

My hope is that here, at the end of this book, you are finding your heart open, and that you have a deeper understanding for Attitudinal Healing. The best way to ensure that the lessons and experiences of this book continue to grow is to practice the principles in your daily life. If ever you can't think of a reason to smile, know that the solution is with you always: Extend love. If you want to smile from your heart, do something that is incredibly kind, with no emphasis on recognition.

Share kindness, compassion, and understanding with those you know and those you don't, and include nature. This is all you need to do to smile.

> *May we all smile upon each
> other and know we are loved.*

Hampton Roads Publishing Company
... for the evolving human spirit

HAMPTON ROADS PUBLISHING COMPANY
publishes books on a variety
of subjects, including, spirituality,
health, and other related topics.

For a copy of our latest trade catalog,
call toll-free, 800-766-8009,
or send your name and address to:

HAMPTON ROADS PUBLISHING COMPANY, INC.
1125 STONEY RIDGE ROAD • CHARLOTTESVILLE, VA 22902
E-mail: hrpc@hrpub.com • Internet: www.hrpub.com